First paperback edition April 2024

Book design by Rebecca Morassutti & Zai Tayebaly

ISBN 979-8-9894171-0-0 | ISBN 979-8-9894171-1-7

www.WendyYellen.com

GRACEFULLY UNLEASHED
YOUR JOURNEY OF DEEP TRANSFORMATION

By
Wendy Yellen

Table Of Contents

INTRODUCTION

"There is a crack in everything. That's how the light gets in."

-Leonard Cohen

She sat with her arms crossed, insisting she wanted to change, while everything in her posture screamed "NO!" But she had driven an hour in traffic to get here and she said she wanted to feel differently. I took her at her word. Her posture and the dense energetic heaviness of her body added fuel to the *no*. Her *no* demanded attention. And I also felt the tender ache of yearning in her *yes*. I knew the work in front of us was to get beyond, behind or through that wall of *no*.

If you've ever tried to help someone who resisted your efforts, you know it's exasperating. They ask for help, so why won't they listen? The simple reason is that human beings rarely act logically.

Why then do we keep trying to help ourselves and others with logic?

Some friends and loved ones give up and walk away. Some fearless people keep trying. But whatever the result, you know what it feels like to help someone who says *yes* and *no* at the same time. Even more important, you know what it feels like to try to wriggle out of your own locked box of *no* when you also want to say *yes*.

In some systems of therapy, the work is to help a client to

understand why they want to repeatedly and loudly say *no* instead of *yes*. In other systems the therapist "prescribes the symptom." They tell the client to do the resistant thing—keep saying no, in the hopes that their oppositional nature will then allow them to actually do the thing they say they *want* to do. Other body-based systems encourage the client to feel their way through.

Now what about you? Have you ever known the best action for you to take and then, inexplicably, not been able to get yourself to do it? We all have. That's the human condition. Ironic, seemingly misguided, insanely frustrating—and rampant. From New Year's resolutions (which are MIA before February) to desperate promises to be more patient and loving with our children (promises which are forgotten at the first tantrum), it is our resistance to what we *say* we want that is the stumbling block to change.

Deal with resistance, and you open the doorway for change to walk in, sit down, and become your best friend. How?

By working with that resistance on a different level of our consciousness.

And after almost 45 years of using traditional and non-traditional forms of therapy, I knew that this deep level of consciousness was what I and my clients craved to create deep transformation in our lives. I have had (and still have) the privilege and honor of working with people who sense there is more to life than they've experienced and who choose to do the work required to move beyond familiar old patterns that hold them back. I've always felt a responsibility to meet their desire and give them the best methodologies I could find.

"The difference between you and the blessed beast of your nature is what you remember of things and what things really are."

~Akhter Ahsen, Father of Eidetic Imagery Therapy

Disclaimer: Every story in this book is true, although many details have been changed to protect my clients' privacy. Every reader, including my clients, will find a piece of yourself in every story. Most of the stories are of women because now most of my clients are women, but I've worked with many men who benefit as well.

A bit about me: I received my Masters in Social Work from Smith College School for Social Work in 1981, was one of two people selected for a year-long Family Therapy Fellowship and went on to be trained and certified in a variety of other traditional and non-traditional therapeutic modalities. I found Eidetic imagery out of personal desperation, and when I understood what was changing in me, I embraced it fully, letting go of all the other modalities I knew. Dr. Ahsen, the father of Eidetic Imagery Therapy, trained and mentored me personally. During almost 45 years of experience working with my clients, I created the Deep Transformation Method™ because in my experience only deep inner work can create meaningful, real and lasting change.

What's different about this work: Many times, people who have done a great deal of other therapies tell me: I never knew this could happen, I've never had this happen before, I didn't know this was (still) there in me. This knowing of what is truly possible, this profound experience of the deeper self waiting for us, this is why I do this work, and why I wrote this book for you.

I'll start with some basic concepts to give you a sense of the work.

About Eidetics

"We seek the fire of the spark that is already within us."

~ Kamand Kojouri

In the same way that describing an orgasm doesn't even approximate the intensity or pleasure of the actual experience, it's difficult to describe an Eidetic image process. Yet, I'd like to give you a sense of it, so I'll be describing several client experiences in the pages that follow.

An Eidetic image is an image formed at important moments in your life, both positive and negative. It can be vivid or vague, it has feelings and emotions attached, and multiple layers of meaning. It is not a visualization or guided image.

Within your painful past is you *without* your history, the *real* you. You don't imagine this real you. You don't fantasize "what if there was a different me," or imagine if you went back and talked to your younger self, or any other fantasy or conscious corrective experience of what could have been. This is one of the hardest concepts for people to grasp, since there is nothing to compare it to, no matter how much personal work you've done.

The ancient Greeks, who gave us incredible innovations and concepts like gymnasiums, columns that have withstood earthquakes, diagnostic medicine, the Olympic games, and citizen input into government, also understood the value of Eidetic images and called them "gifts from the gods."[1]

It's important to understand the difference between fantasy and an Eidetic image. When you have a fantasy of a wonderful life, it's more like a wish that you elaborate on.

It often has feelings of wistfulness or a dream, and you don't really believe it or find it likely to happen, "If I won the lottery, I would be happy." It contains desire, but nothing solid, and it is not felt as a reality, it feels like an "if only" or "wouldn't that be great?" An Eidetic image is something quite different.

You may *wish* your parents treated you differently, you may *wish* you could feel less conflict with your daughter, you may *wish* for a holiday without family strife, but those wishes don't feel real. They are wishes, not experiences. When you are present to your life (and not wishing you felt different), you *live in* actual life experiences. You sit down and look at your beloved and thank the powers that be that they are sitting next to you, greying and lined, perhaps, but here. You inhale their scent and feel their energy. It gives you pleasure and brings memories. You feel kindness in your belly and you feel totally yourself.

An Eidetic image feels that real.

To *know* an Eidetic image, it's necessary to have one. I can describe it, but there is nothing like the actual experience. I can tell you what Talenti Sea Salt Caramel ice cream tastes like, but you can only approximate the pleasure, until you take a bite. (If you are an ice cream lover, I recommend it! It's that good.) To have your own Eidetic *experience*, and to help you know more about yourself and lay a great foundation for what you can receive from the book in your hands, you can find one here as my gift to you: www.WendyYellen.com/DTMBook.

---

1 The word Eidetics comes from the Greek word Eidos, meaning form or essence, something that is seen or intuited. (Merriam Webster Dictionary). Eidetic Imagery Therapy is different from "eidetic memory", which is similar to a photographic memory.

"But the mind already has the ability to heal itself."

The body has the ability to heal itself, but we assume the mind does not. Instead, we assume we have to use our logic to control and "fix" our mind and force it to act correctly. If someone is healthy and they cut their finger and they keep it clean, the cut normally heals on its own. We don't convince the cut to heal. That's unnecessary. Our body knows what to do without our mind's logic interfering.[2]

Yet we don't believe that our psyche has a similar inner mechanism for healing itself as the body does. So, we utilize our logic and emotions in an attempt to heal the distress within our psyche.

But the mind already has the ability to heal itself. It's powerful, it's life-giving. You find this healing power within your deeper mind, your Eidetic consciousness. Many people do experience shifts and changes using a logic-oriented or emotion-oriented process. Personally, I needed something more. Something more for me, and something more for my clients.

Simply put, instead of *starting* with thinking or *starting* with feelings, in my eight stage process called the Deep Transformation Method™ (DTM) and using the tool of Eidetics we start with that deep level of consciousness, our Eidetic Consciousness. At this level, there are unique-to-each-person images which are formed at important times in our life, times of trauma or wonder. Each Eidetic image contains an image, feelings, and multiple layers of meaning, and we all have them. *Starting* the change process with these images, instead of starting with thinking or feeling, is the

---

2 Yes, the mind can help with healing but it's not through logic or force. The healing power of the mind is from its deeper levels of consciousness.

difference that makes *all* the difference.

Einstein tells us that you can't solve a problem on the same level at which it was created. You've heard this and it makes intuitive sense. I don't know what Einstein would say in this specific situation, but I can give you some ideas from almost 45 years of meeting my clients on the battlefield between resistance and desire. What most of us want is permanent inner transformation, the kind

> **"We want to be unleashed, but the way we think we have to do it makes the leash tighten around our neck."**

where you shock yourself by acting and feeling so differently in a situation that has been challenging for you all your life.

Transformation this deep won't happen if you stay on the same level at which your problem was created.

The most familiar two levels of problem solving interventions are 1) changing how you think and 2) changing how you feel.

If you think and feel that you are someone who is less-than—who is not truly loveable, who doesn't really deserve to shine in the world, who can't succeed, who can never find love, who can't change your marriage from ships passing in the night, who can't get yourself to treat yourself well—those problems are already *deep* within the way you think and the way you feel about yourself.

My best educated guess is that Einstein would say that you can't solve the thoughts you're thinking by thinking them away and you can't resolve the emotions you're feeling by trying to feel them away. If you try to change a thought by thinking another thought, your intervention is on the same level as the problem. If you have a feeling that cripples you, such as "I am not enough" and you try to force that feeling away or try to fake it 'til you make it, you are working to change feelings at the level of feelings.

When we try to resolve our difficult or incorrect thinking and feeling at the same level they were created, it's like chasing a flooding river with a broom, yelling "Stop!"

We want to be unleashed, but the way we think we have to do it makes the leash tighten around our neck.

The Problem with Logic

"To go beyond all knowledge is to find that comprehension which eludes the mind."

~Attar, Sufi poet

Let's start with how people normally go about addressing a problem: with logic. The problem with logic goes back to Einstein's insight that you can't solve a problem on the level at which it was created.

When confronted with a problem, it's common to point a finger outward to blame other people or circumstances. But once you realize that the resolution of the issue must come from within yourself, then you have an opportunity for your own growth. You probably first do your best to change how you think or feel about it. You feel angry at your adult daughter, so you do your best to stop being angry at her. When you are with your sister, you think what she is doing is foolish, so you do your best to stop thinking about her that way so you can get along. We tend to understand the problem as originating in our thinking or our feelings ("I am wrong to think this way. I don't want to feel this way.") so it makes sense from that point of view to try to change those thoughts and feelings.

One of the underlying but hidden assumptions in this

orientation to solving problems is that it assumes we don't contain within us another more organic, powerful and successful way to shift how we are being. It gives the so-called rational mind precedence and a lot of weight. It assumes that our logical mind can prevail, that we are logical creatures who simply need a soft prod to get us back on track. If we realize we are off, we think we can self-correct by simply getting ourselves to think and feel differently.

Has that been your experience? Do you see the world around you acting rationally most of the time? Have you ever panicked during an upheaval of the stock market and sold at exactly the wrong moment? Have you ever felt ashamed at how you behaved when you knew better? Have you ever wondered why we, as a species, are so careless and abusive with our planet as if we could simply relocate to another one?

People don't use logic as our primary modality to navigate life. I don't think Spock of Star Trek fame would have been as fascinating to us if he hadn't been an anomaly, unique because of his intensely logical mind. The writers of the show even softened Spock's logic by giving him a mother who came from Earth, a mother who, based on her origins, was not logical by default.

Many forms of therapy and personal growth work assume that we are logical beings and if we understood our behavior we would simply stop. Very little about human beings is logical. We are busy poisoning the only planet we have to live on. Couples connect and then hurt or even murder each other. People start good eating programs and exercise or yoga and a month later it's a distant wish. We hire coaches and therapists and ignore or delay what they suggest. And so much more. We are not logical. Any process that is meant to create real change on a bedrock level must include this basic understanding about us as humans.

And the mind also has its own way of dealing with life that dismisses the richness of our experience. When you see an unusual bird, you delight in its beauty and its haunting song. You feel a deep pleasure and connection with nature. Then you look up the name of the bird, "Ah… that's a Canyon Wren", and the mind takes over: "OK, that's a Canyon Wren. Got it. Next!" The mind receives a satisfaction from knowing the name. The experience of the bird is now in the shorthand of something we "know." It's compartmentalized and categorized. "I got it! Let's move on."

But what do we know through the mind? We know the name. What about the way that lyrical song touched the heart, softened something in us, reminded us of a rafting trip through canyons dripping with waterfalls newly created by the thunderstorm we just

"What you want is a resolution, not a repetition."

rafted through? That we were soaked to the bone but enchanted. The mind short-circuits all of that, sweeps it aside and says, "Got it! Next!"

Our world rewards this way of using the mind. Quick, short, impatient, efficient yet usually superficial. It's as satisfying as a sugar jolt and is equally as empty of nourishment. The mind runs much of our daily lives while so many of us crave the deeper meaning we find in meditation, yoga, and spiritual practices. Part of us *knows* we need something deeper than the mind's shorthand.

What happens in relationships when we come from the efficient, impatient energy of the mind? We feel jittery: "I know that already. Move on!" How can we experience the depth of our partner when we can't slow down? When we're so wrapped in the mind's irritation about how long it takes them to get to the point?

But what is the point? Is the point of what they are saying that there was a lot of traffic, or they had a bad day, or a client was difficult? Or is the deeper point that they want to be with you, to tell you about what is on their mind, to connect with you? To *feel your presence with them?*

Perhaps the "point of the story" they are trying to tell is the desire for an oceanic feeling of contact with someone who sees, knows, and loves them. And when you are irritated or impatiently waiting for "the point", how can they feel that from you? How can *you* feel that from you? It's not possible. Those deeper states of being can't be contacted from hurry or impatience.

How does this "quick conclusion without real depth" connect with transformational work? That impatience, that not really listening when you think you are, not really thinking because you are moving too fast, not really being with what *is* rather than what you *assume* is there—all of this leaps over deep transformation to get to some point which isn't the point but which satisfies us with some semblance of "Next"!

"Reason's eyes will never glimpse one spark of shining love to mitigate the dark."

~Attar, Sufi poet

Emotions

So, starting with our overly-impatient thinking mind will not work. And when we start with our *feelings* about a situation to solve a problem we *inadvertently fall back into our often-repeated historical reactions and feelings.* These are responses which aren't serving us now but, because they feel oh-so-familiar, they seem somehow right. When you rely on a feeling to steer you in the right direction and that feeling is hitched to your historical reactions to similar problems, you lose access to the best of your problem-solving abilities. You only get more of the same old answers and reactions that have never been successful in the past. What you want is a resolution, not a repetition.

When the obstacle, the resistance, is inside you, it's all you know and all-consuming. Let's take hurt, anger and pain in relationships as an example. Yes, you can take a step, one that feels better and more open, and forgive. Yes, you can do your best to overlook the hurtful slights of your partner or stuff the hurt back inside. Yes, you can tell yourself you don't want to hurt them. But what does that do for you—or them—in the end? Does that change who you are and what you are perhaps feeling that you have instead hidden or repressed? Does that allow you to give your partner the love you, and they, ache for?

My client Brian[3] told me he was working hard to be less critical towards his wife. He was holding back his criticism and anger towards her so they could have a kinder, more loving relationship. Yet, he had enough insight to realize that, though this behavior kept him from hurling knee-jerk, hurtful judgmental barbs at her, *it didn't make him feel more loving to his wife.* He successfully held himself back from criticizing and judging her even though it was what he felt inside but didn't want to express to her for fear of hurting her. However, it didn't open his heart more to his wife. And, at bottom, that was what he ardently wanted.

Bonnie Raitt sang a line that is so perfect: "You can't make your heart feel something it won't." If you've ever tried to force yourself to love someone you wished you could love, you know how true that is. *It's near impossible to force yourself to feel a way you don't.*

---

3 All client names and personal details have been changed for their privacy.

Neuroplasticity:
White Water Rafting Down the Grand Canyons of Your Brain

"Being defensive and uptight, lazy, irritable, or self-conscious—these behaviors are not in our DNA and do not have to continue their destructive influence. They can die before we do."

~ *Yongey Mingyur Rinpoche*

You couldn't easily describe the steps to tie your walking shoes, and you may not remember in detail how you got from the grocery store to your house, but your brain knows the way. Think of these common actions as deeply worn grooves in your brain. They are time-saving, energy-saving shortcuts for often—repeated thoughts, memories and patterns. Because they've been used frequently, the bits of information and instructions move quickly along a well-traveled neural pathway without the additional delay that would come from wondering, "Now what do I do next?" No conscious thought is needed. You can get into your car or put on a pair of pants without thinking about which leg goes in first.

The neural pathways for our knee-jerk reactions to people, challenges and situations run deep. Tap the knee in a certain place and it immediately jerks without any forethought. Touch a hot stove and your hand jerks away without any conscious instruction. Our knee-jerk reactions to life's challenges make us respond in the same way we've always responded. That doesn't make those responses helpful or even adequate. But they are, at least, familiar.

Sue, a mother of teenagers, and a professional in her late 50's, called me to discuss possibly working together so she could "reconnect to myself, I've been so far away from me for decades and it's time to change that."

But even though she urgently *wanted* to feel better in her own skin, when we tried to find a time to meet and get started, nothing worked. Everything and everyone pulled on her time so much that she literally could not find a single hour to meet. She was so conditioned to responding to others' needs that she felt she had no choice but to continue doing so—even though it meant she didn't have the time to pursue what she knew she needed for herself.

I have clients who video-call me from their cars in order to have privacy because of work or family situations. Some women drive to a quiet beach or park to have some peace during our work. That's commitment. People close the door in an office or meeting room, during their lunch hour, with a Do Not Disturb sign on the door. Women make sure their partners understand that even if what they are doing makes no sense to their spouse, it makes sense to them. They commit to having a better life—including their marriage! Not all of this came easily, but they all find a way.

Sue *wanted* to change, but her deep, knee-jerk patterns in response to other people pulling on her made finding *time for herself impossible*. This needed to be addressed in order to even have our first private session.

Sue had travelled down the neuropathway of "I don't have time for me" so often that it became her default position.

The *feeling* (and the thought) she had was that it was impossible to carve out time for herself because the mind-numbing demands on her left no time or energy. This pattern isn't sustainable—at least not while keeping your sanity! You cannot continue on an empty tank without refilling it. Even with the best intentions, you cannot truly give of yourself if you have nothing left to give. Some part of Sue needed to truly know that before we even started.

Fortunately, those urges from deep inside that *something* needed to change allowed her to advocate on her own behalf and actually find a time to get started.

There's a beautiful forest trail near Santa Fe which is so popular during autumn Aspen season that it feels like a boulevard. That's how I think of our well-worn neural pathways. Wide, well-traveled, and clear from lots of use over many years of living. Conversely, there are trails that almost no one ever uses. With little use, they seem to disappear into a no-man's land of thorny brambles, and fallen limbs, and this debris makes the trail almost invisible. The path is still there, but it's cluttered and not easy to find or use. These are like the neural pathways that, although they are still in our brains, the synapses haven't been fired frequently, so they aren't an *automatic path* for our thoughts or actions.

What does this have to do with deep inner change, with feeling better about yourself, with having an open heart? *Everything.*

The thoughts of "I'm not enough," "I'm not loveable," "I'll never find a partner I can love," "If they really knew me they wouldn't like me," "I'll never live up to my potential" feel *very* real. But in fact, neurologically, they are simply a well-worn neural pathway in your brain. One of my Mastermind clients says that the *negative* neural pathways in her are so well-traveled and so automatic, they feel like the Grand Canyon. Once she gets down into her personal Grand Canyon hell, the journey is swift and relentless, and takes her to extremely negative, and thoroughly familiar, thoughts and feelings about herself, her value, and her future.

For Sara, a mid-50's, dynamic non-profit executive and single mother, the thoughts and feelings she had all of the time were down a Grand Canyon of "I'm not loveable" which increased until it was almost a self-loathing. Though at times she felt painfully lonely, she avoided dating, interacting with or even allowing herself to feel attracted to eligible men in her sphere. Her sense that she could never be loved or even liked for who she was started affecting her at work. If she had even a whiff of a different thought or feeling about relationships or herself, it quickly disappeared. The mere idea that she had something to contribute and was someone who was loveable did not feel real to her. Her Grand Canyon was that deep and that compelling to her. It was as if nothing else existed inside her but those negative places. The only place of pleasure and relief she found was reading fiction. And even that relief was fleeting.

If you've ever whitewater rafted down the Grand Canyon, you

know how swift and treacherous those rapids can be and how relentless the path downstream is. You can't fight it. It goes where it goes.

That's how the negative thoughts felt to Sara. There was no fighting them. She totally believed these familiar thoughts and feelings about herself. And yet, she desperately, passionately wanted to feel differently about herself. Truly different. Not faking it, not pretend, not superficially. She had tried for decades but she couldn't get there. What *could* allow her to travel honestly down another path? And was there anything besides a novel that could give her respite from the negativity and loneliness? She had hit the point where her body was rebelling and deteriorating before her eyes and needed her to treat it differently.

Those devastatingly negative but familiar Grand Canyon thoughts can't be shifted *on the level* of the Grand Canyon *in which they travel*. What Sara needed was to experience those older, more positive but less-trod and heavily bramble-covered neuropathways she hadn't been down in many decades. The problem was that she didn't believe she had any.

If, like Sara, you aren't sure you have or ever had any positive pathways, hang in there with me. Each person I work with comes to me with the secret belief that *all they have is their treacherous Grand Canyon*. They, you, all of us have access to *other* thoughts and feelings which are already there, buried beneath the crust of your history.[4] Even if you don't believe it yet. You might be thinking, "If I do have them, where *are* they? And worse, why can't I 'feel' them?"

If you *could* travel down one of those positive neural pathways in your brain, how *would* it feel?

The biggest hurdle for Sara was her reliance on her thinking

4   Akhter Ahsen, PhD, father of Eidetic Imagery Therapy, introduced me to this phrase, which I find extremely useful in understanding where our resources are buried.

mind. Whenever her Eidetic images gave her an authentic, embodied and positive feeling, she would negate them with thinking and so-called logic. She would point to the "proof" she had found over the years to argue that her belief that she was not loveable was true. She would think any other possibility away. Each time she did this her body tightened up and her arms crossed in front of her, barricading her.

As I gently guided her to stay with the different leveled process going on inside her, which was coming from deep inside her, she began to trust that there really was another part of her that was loveable and worthy. Over time, her arms uncrossed, and her face softened to an Aphrodite-like beauty. This experience of herself allowed her to feel more satisfaction in her job as she now feels appreciated and liked in her organization. She has also started to enjoy discovering and interacting with potential partners and she finally feels the possibility of pleasure from something besides reading about fictional lives and adventures.

Neuroplasticity allowed Sara to go down a different path. Welcome to the "other level" Einstein pointed us toward. The other level in our psyche and even in our soul.[5]

5 Deep transformational work opens us to our beautiful capacity for presence and awe. After one session, one woman said she felt "transcendental love." This is why I refer to our soul in this book. I don't know what literally happens to us on that level, but I know that the feeling of our soul being nurtured is very common in this work.

Resistance:
Why We Fight
What We Want

Fear is a natural reaction to moving closer to the truth."

~ Pema Chödrön

Remember we talked about resistance, and how we resist what we say we want? That's the Grand Canyon, the well-carved neural pathway. The other pathways are harder to reach, so we go down the more accessible groove time and again. It's all powerful—and often depressing. It's the negative identification with a parent or parents, which we are often insistently blind to. All of these are reasons why finding *you* beneath the crust of your history and traveling down a different neural pathway is so critical to your wellbeing and feeling of aliveness, freedom and expansion. Because

"The way we began, the roads we've taken, the assumptions and holes in our understanding are what determine our destination."

we don't *know* how to find another level to come from, because we are resistant to what we say we want and try to solve it on the same level where the resistance resides, our *efforts* to resolve our own obstacles continue to *contain the seeds of what we don't want.* Our results are then the fruit of the poisoned tree. The way we began, the roads we've taken, the assumptions and holes in our understanding are what determine our destination.

We try to feel differently. We try to act differently. But trying to change behavior alone doesn't contain enough love or enough energy to follow through on commitments to ourselves. We try to think differently but again, it contains the seeds of the old way—the *only* way—we ever learned to think. The only way we ever learned to think about ourselves, our problems, our desires, our abilities has led us to where we are today. We can't solve whatever problems we face from those constrained, inaccurate, less-than-whole parts of ourselves. And so, what we are using as the solution continues to contain the problem inside of it. Which means we never really get away from the problem.

One of my clients, Carole, a highly skilled, insightful and empathic business owner, almost never felt good about herself, "I am not enough. What I do is wrong. No one can really love me." Feeling this way about herself, she resisted all efforts to compliment or assure her. She struggled to feel and do better, and never took pleasure from what she was *already* doing that was excellent. Without realizing it, this Achilles heel of not-good-enough seeped into her leadership style. Instead of leading her employees from her excellent qualities of empathy and intelligence and caring, she unconsciously tried to get her staff to like her and respect her.

Her employees could feel it even if they could not articulate it. This energy of "Please, *please* like me!" undermined her authority, her presence, her ability to thoughtfully lead her company. Unconsciously, she framed her decisions based on whether an action or a statement would increase their respect and liking of her. And since no level of respect or liking of her by her team could truly touch the wound in her, she rejected any appreciation they did give her.

"So how do you solve a problem except with the tools, the thinking and the feelings that you've been using until now?"

This vicious circle can't be *deeply* undone simply by awareness. Like Brian, who couldn't open his heart to his wife but *could* hold back from being so critical, Carole needed more than awareness. She needed a tool to help her feel love for herself, so she wasn't desperate to get it from others. She needed a way to stop resisting what she wanted, and instead to be able to feel the love and appreciation *already* coming to her.

So how *do* you solve a problem except with the tools, the thinking and the feelings that you've been using until now? Different forms of therapy and personal growth think they have the answer.

The common thought now is to change how you feel or how you think. How would that work for Carol?

She might have been encouraged to understand that, of course, she is loveable. "Obviously everyone is loveable. Why wouldn't you be? Just because you were different and your parents tried to make you fit into the family, doesn't make you a bad person." This is the "change your thinking, be more logical" approach. Or she might have been encouraged to *feel* differently. "Look in the mirror and tell yourself 'I love you.'" "You don't have to feel this way. You can feel another way. Just feel it and you will feel better." Or how about the infamous, "Fake it 'til you make it!"?

When I was a young woman, I went to a workshop where the well-meaning facilitators sat each of us in front of our own

> *"But for me, and I suspect for you,*
> *the way out must be real."*

mirror, and encouraged us, one-on-one, to do just that. I was supposed to say, "I love you Wendy" into my reflection. I refused. I wouldn't lie to myself, and I would not say something to myself that I did NOT mean. Every word of that statement felt like a lie, and being asked to say it while feeling the lie of it made me feel worse. Much worse.

Was I being resistant to what I most wanted? Absolutely. I did want to love myself. But for me, and I suspect for you, the way out *must be real.*

I don't just believe, I *know* that there is a place inside of me, of you, of everyone, that is organically, naturally, breath-takingly whole. Not in some fantasy world, not pie-in-the-sky, not pretend. Real. And I also know that this part of you is already there and begging, heart-bursting, yearning, to get out. And, paradoxically, all of us will fight against this part even harder than she can fight to get out. Some call this a form of self-defeat or self-sabotage. I call it resistance to what you want the most.

When, with the best intentions, we impose restrictions on this buried but organically whole part inside, she rebels. And for good reason. When you try to manacle her, tame her into submission, she often frantically lashes out until you feel her discomfort, anger and disappointment. You'll continue to feel less than who you hope you really are until she gets released into your life bringing all her positive potentials. The fact that you feel uncomfortable is a powerful clue that something wonderful in you isn't currently accessible to you. But are there possibly other levels of how to change that could be more accessible, understandable, or practical that can circumvent our resistance? Other levels beyond thinking and feeling that could create the deep, organic transformation you need? What new levels do we have to reach?

I worked with a 50+ year-old professional, Ann, with lots of letters behind her name and such a tenacity on behalf of her clients that they brought her some of the toughest situations in her field. During our work together, she experienced "an incredible, intense, glorious, wonderful feeling of playfulness and desire" that made her feel whole. At the end of one session, she said, "I actually am able to savor this feeling." These states of being came from deep inside of her and shocked her. She had never been able to savor a positive feeling in her adult life. Yet despite experiencing this glorious feeling, what did she focus on *instead*? She focused on her sadness that she hadn't been experiencing this awesome feeling up until then!

In the very moment that she found something new, fresh, different, real and profoundly important to her, she focused on the fact that she hadn't been feeling it before.

Our minds can't focus on two things at the exact same moment, and so the focus on what she'd *not had* overwhelmed the newly discovered radiant part of her. She felt so sad.

Let's tease this apart, because her story sheds light on what we humans do.

CR

Is it true that Ann had not felt these powerful emotions before? Yes. Certainly not to this degree, and not with this focus and awareness. Noticing that and feeling sad that she hadn't experienced this before is a natural and an authentic reaction.

But instead of simply noting her sadness and going back to the Eidetic process that gave her access to that dazzling feeling and state of being that she craved, Ann stayed focused on what she hadn't had in the decades before. She focused on sadness.

It's a graphic, common story. You are having the deepest, boldest, whole-body-mind-soul orgasm of your life. Right at that moment, your mind remembers you haven't had this kind of orgasm before. You spend the rest of the orgasm (and the evening and maybe the next several days) thinking about how you never had an orgasm like this before. What a waste of time and energy, right? You lose the moment. There is only one Now and you can only be here now. You've heard this. You've experienced this. It makes sense to you. And you also know that it's *so* hard to let go of this tendency for the mind to go back to what you *didn't* have, what you *didn't* feel, what you *didn't* do, what they *didn't* say to you, et cetera.

Why do you go back there? It's that well-worn path of

feeling unfulfilled and unhappy. Even after you experience new neuropathways, as freeing as they are, they don't have the pull on you that the old ones have—*yet*. By working with the Eidetic images, new pathways become more natural and familiar until the old hellish Grand Canyons become places you can barely remember.[6]

I'll share one of my personal experiences with resisting what I wanted the most. I feel strange even telling you this, but I also know that this, or something like it, goes on with all of us.

For years, I had the extraordinary privilege to work directly with Dr. Akhter Ahsen, the father of Eidetic Imagery Therapy. We worked by phone, and I also flew across the country to see him for several two-day private intensives at his office in New York. Akhter was a Renaissance man and visionary with a breadth of knowledge and interest you rarely come across anymore. Among other things, he was a deep thinker, poet, philosopher, PhD psychologist, and author of dozens of books and hundreds of journal articles. Instead of the one-idea books we often find today, in his books, each paragraph contained thoughts and ideas and depth that your mind could take in, wrestle with, learn from and grow with. He understood the deeper mind and what we are capable of in a way which sang to my soul. Finally, here was someone who understood how real change happens and could take me there!

From my first year at Smith College School for Social Work in 1979, to my Master's Thesis on how transformation occurs, I was hungry to know how people change. In Dr. Ahsen, I had found the Holy Grail! I flew from New Mexico to New York about four times a year for several years to study and work with him. I took

my most challenging clients to him for consultation and they all remember the experience with gratitude and love to this day.

And yet...

6   One of the fun aspects about DTM and Eidetics is that often a client will not even remember what the chaotic or disturbing situation was that we worked with Eidetically the week before. This is an astonishing aspect of how deep, meaningful change manifests in our lives.

In my personal work, I worked hard *not* to let in him, and *not* to let in the work. How odd! I had found the answer to my prayers, he was teaching me and working with me personally, and still I automatically *resisted* feeling better!

It showed up like this: We would work together on the phone. Based on my Consciousness Mapping, he would choose images specifically for me to open up to more business success and more ease in my life, to allow less constriction and soften my automatic No's. He would give me an Eidetic image to use and we would work with it together. I would see and feel it. It would break through my history to the part of me that actually felt good. And what was my response? Did I smile, thank him, enjoy the energy coursing through me? No, I would not. Instead, I would hide my good feelings from him! It was shocking to me to watch it happen. Here I was, paying his consulting fee (which for me at the time was a stretch), and spending all this time and energy to feel better. Then, I would get there, I would repress the better feeling in my voice and *not* show it. Ostensibly, I was hiding it from him but, of course, I was hiding it from myself too.

While I knew at the time it was ridiculous, it was also automatic. I struggled to find a way to allow myself to let him know (if only through the inflections in my voice) that the work was helping me. I felt the changes flash through my body, lighting up my very being, and I *wanted* him to know.

Yet I'm glad I experienced this because my own resistance to change allows me now to understand how we *all* resist in our unique ways. The experience gave me both empathy and knowledge of how to work with it.

If you don't work with your resistance to change, you can't achieve real change. When you *soften* resistance to the change that you want and the mind repeatedly experiences this change, then you are automatically harnessing the power of neuroplasticity to create new pathways. These new pathways become your new default mode of feeling and behaving. Use a system that deals with your resistance to change and the real you will emerge organically.

Parental Identification:
Forming Crusts
of History

I mentioned the crusts of history that we need to dissolve to uncover the organic Self inside you that is filled with potential. That crust is made up of two main aspects: parental identity and your filters. Though the two are slightly different and worked with differently in the Deep Transformation Method™ they tend to overlap. It's not as important to understand their differences as to understand the impact they have on your life.

When I took my highly successful, locally based private practice of psychotherapy into the international arena, using the tool of Eidetics, I didn't have a clue how to tell people about this work and what it could do. My early training and business successes had come relatively easily to me. While that was wonderful, it meant that I didn't know or understand that many parts of me were stubborn and seemingly bound and determined to get into my own way. It was a shock to come face to face with them!

Since then, it has become obvious to me that when most people expand or aim for a new height in their work life, or when they open their own business to become an entrepreneur, or when they change careers entirely, every single part of them that seemingly resists their own best interests will come out and interfere with that greater success.

That's what happened to me.

Years ago, I hired a high-ticket business coach. If she suggested (and I agreed) that I would benefit from, say, contacting 20 new people a week for possible alliances for marketing, I would contact two or three, if that. It's not that I had better things to do, and it's not that I thought it was a bad idea. But week after week, I delayed. If this was the most important action my highly paid and well-respected business coach suggested to me, and I wanted to have a more successful business, you would think those 20 contacts would be the *first* thing I would do each week.

Well, it wasn't. Week after week after week I would delay, procrastinate, and generally act as if it wasn't important. If I was going to ignore her expert advice, what was I paying her for?

Strange as it sounds, I was barely even *aware* that I wasn't doing what I had agreed to do. I had a strange feeling in my gut most of the time, but I thought that was because the coaching "wasn't working" and I wasn't seeing my business grow quickly enough.

The heart of my resistance to focusing in a useful way in my business was by *unconsciously acting like my father*. I loved and still love my father. He had some great philanthropic and visionary qualities, but he also went bankrupt several times. He had a hard time with details and especially with following through and getting the train to the station on important projects.

I didn't *know* I was acting like him, but in hindsight it is completely obvious. Pay close attention here because you will likely find several parts of yourself in my story.

Like my father, instead of working to complete the tasks my coach suggested, I created a beautiful home study course with multiple CDs, a thorough and easy to follow workbook, long sales pages and a beautiful full-color cover. I had no idea if anyone would want to buy this course, but I *loved* creating it. I *knew* better than to put months into creating something which would probably attract very few buyers, I *knew* that my time would be better spent following my coach's advice to grow my business first, but *I didn't do it.*

I was resistant to doing the very thing that would bring me what I wanted most. And I had no idea I was being so resistant! I thought I was being creative and making a difference.

This is different from being resistant to success, which is a phrase that is often used in business coaching. Let's tease it out. I wasn't afraid of success. I wanted financial success, I wanted to make a bigger difference in the world. I also knew I could do both, because I had done both before, when I was working in the smaller arena of Houston, Texas, rather than internationally.

But internally, there were templates in my deeper consciousness that, like a siren song, seduced me to "Go this way, go this way." I followed these destructive templates without consciously knowing I was doing it. They would have led to disaster if I hadn't done some real, deep, sometimes painful work. One of the most insidious parts in me insisted on being blind to what I was doing, *even though several very caring people went way out of their way to show me in black and white the destructive paths I was on and how dangerous it was to keep doing what I was doing.* I could not listen. I would not listen. Only through the deep work of unhitching myself from this negative identification through Eidetics was I able to take in what was so obvious to others.

No matter how many times my coach suggested the same strategy of 20-30 calls, she couldn't get me to do it. As strange as it may sound now, I was oblivious to this glaring hole in my thinking and actions. At the time, Dr. Akhter Ahsen told me that I was *practicing being like my father.* This sent shudders down my body because I knew how that story played out. Still, it took me a long time to stop.

If all of us were logical creatures as human beings, I would have followed her advice immediately. But we aren't, so I didn't. And no amount of pure logic was going to help me let go of being creative to make those calls and connections to new potential alliances instead.

And if you are shaking your head and saying "I wouldn't have wanted to make those calls either" let me add this. Once I started making those contacts in earnest, one of the many fun, surprising perks and successes that followed included being invited to present an "Evening with Wendy" to a small group of women in the Hill District of England (and I tacked on a solo trip to Morocco—but that's another story), and multiple invites and encore invites for "Evenings with Wendy" in the heart of Manhattan, near Boston and Washington, DC, just to name a few. Each one challenged me to the max. I was crazy nervous before each one, but I also had a great time, and met dozens of motivated, exceptional women who became my clients. Success was ready to show up once I got out of my own way.

But back then I was still determined to stand in my own way. I was practicing being like my father in the area most important to me at the time—*the financial and international success of my psychotherapy practice.* I didn't follow through with the details that my business coach suggested for years! I wandered off on alluring tangents that were delicious and also useless. I ignored the state of my finances. I ignored the wise counsel that my successful younger sister tried hard to give me.

All of this had to do with my negative identification with my father. It wasn't conscious. I was being "insistently blind" to my inner obstacles. But, my goodness, did it show up in my business *results!* In the midst of avoiding what I needed to do, I was swept up in waves of shame and fear. How could I be getting in my way so badly when I had so many resources and skills and excellent training and plenty of initials behind my name?

I had another, very different identification with my mother. This one is ironic and sad to me. My mother was competent, efficient, effective and beautiful. But her superpowers came at a cost. She felt an unyielding drive for perfection and intense shame when she didn't meet that goal. She never felt good enough. And inadvertently, she passed that need to be perfect along to me.

It would have been *great* for me to have *her* abilities in my work, but not at the cost of a thin-lipped driven intensity that felt oppressive to me. So, I ran unconsciously in the other direction.

For me, the other direction was identification with my father's appealing visionary side.

In doing so, I lost my connection with my mother's abilities, which would have made success easier, and I attached myself to my father's attractive and also undermining qualities.

I disconnected from effectiveness and attached to not getting the train to the station. Recipe for disaster.

Everyone does something like this. We all have some kind of hidden identification or opposition to our parents. It doesn't matter if they are living or gone, if you have a loving relationship or not. These identifications are inside of us, running the show beneath our conscious awareness.

And oddly we will fight to *keep* our negative identifications, our crust of history. Without realizing it, I was deep into resistance against what I said I wanted. I fought for my limitations. I kicked and screamed when someone tried to show me a way out. This is what we humans do. This goes on inside all of us to some degree and it's why you might feel frustrated by your lack of progress in what matters most.

Experience for Yourself...

Although this applies to any area of your life, let's take a look at what you are suffering from now in one area, your career or work life. Lack of more expansive success? Delay and procrastination? Lack of careful attention to details? Big dreams but mediocre implementation? Feelings of being passed over? Notice the way *you* feel right now. Write it down.

Reflect on each of your parents. Forget about how things feel *now* with your parent(s). Did either one of them suffer from the same problem at some point? Write it down. Did either one go the *opposite* way *toward* massive success, great attention to details, etc.? Write that down, too.

Most likely, any way in which you act like one parent that impacts you negatively is a negative identification. You may be insistently blind to this and object to what I am saying. But if you look at your current results compared to where you desire to be, some truth may reveal itself—*if* you are willing to consider truth that is often *extremely* disturbing.

If you have a parent with resources that you *aren't* expressing, then you may be acting in opposition to what that parent *can* offer you internally. You may need these qualities, and certainly they would help you. But for personal reasons unique to you, possibly related to some rejection of or emotional distance from that parent, you reject these resources. Likely you don't know you are doing this. It's unconscious.

Fortunately, the qualities in the parent whose resources would help you are *already inside of you*. Yes, that is correct, even though you may find that very hard to believe right now. You probably *wish* you could live from those qualities and could express them naturally. You probably feel like you have to *force* yourself to live those qualities. But that feeling that you have to "force yourself" is there because of the way you are currently *not connected* to those parts of you. You are blocked by the crusts of family history, family legend, society and schooling. Even religion and ethnicity can play a part in teaching us what is accepted or expected from us and what is not.

When I looked at my mother achieving so much but being tight-lipped and carrying the weight of perfectionism within everything she did, I didn't want to be like her. I didn't realize how, unconsciously, by rejecting her intense and judgmental introspection, I also rejected *within me* the qualities of effectiveness and efficiency and getting the train to the station—all qualities I needed so much.

There was a feeling of *resistance to being like her*, because of *how* she was in life. I had no idea that I was rejecting her positive qualities too. It was not a conscious decision or conscious desire. And, even worse, I was unconsciously *adamant* about rejecting her. I would not allow any other perspective. Not my sister's loving input, or my husband's observations or my business coach's guidance. I needed to open my mind to the deeper places of resistance that were running the Wendy show.

Note: When we talk about parents, remember that it doesn't matter how you feel or think about them now. It doesn't matter what you remember or even what you think happened in your history. The *way* you remember, and the images inside you defining how things must be and how you are allowed or forced to feel, these are what are running the show.

Why do we fight to keep our identifications? For me, I didn't want to be tight and perfectionistic like my mother. I loved my father's visionary side which was expansive and creative and fun. But since it was all unconscious, I couldn't choose. I didn't know I could retain my father's positive qualities without adopting the negative. I *needed* more of my mother's gifts to get where I wanted to go. But I rejected all her qualities, the good and the bad. I didn't know I was doing this. I didn't know I could access some of her gifts inside me *without acting exactly like her.*

Experience for Yourself:
Finding
Your Identifications

I t's not easy to identify what we are insistently blind to. That's the nature of the beast. Here are five places you can begin to investigate. Writing your answers down will help you because you'll see the connections more clearly:

What do you want that is eluding you right now? Do you feel like you have been and done everything needed at work or in your business, yet you are still not succeeding in the ways you imagine you could?

Is there anything you believe or know that you should be doing

"Who are you practicing being like, even though you don't want to be?"

that you aren't, no matter how much you think it would help?

Are there well-meaning, knowledgeable, experienced folks who've been telling you the same thing repeatedly and you've been rejecting it? Write down their suggestions, even if you don't agree.

What were some of the negative symptoms, behaviors, feelings and beliefs that your mother held? That your father had? Write them down.

Do you have any of the same negative symptoms, behaviors, feelings and beliefs that your mother held? That your father had? Write them down.

This exercise can bring you enormous insight if you can be excruciatingly honest with yourself, though you may still not quite "get" it. That's okay. It's a process. It also takes courage. And it reaps enormous rewards when you find that courage.

Once you've honestly responded to the exercises above, you'll have a better idea, even if you can't quite see it yet, of the ways you are getting in your own way.

You've at least somewhat identified what you want that is eluding you in business or work. (And you can go back and do the same with any other area of your life where you feel dissatisfied and unfulfilled.) You've noticed how a parent acted or felt the same way, and possibly how a parent acted and felt the opposite. Who are you being like? Expressed in a more devastating but pointed way: Who are you practicing being like, even though you don't want to be?

Now we have the key to what stops you from moving forward, that hidden internal resistance to what you say you want in work or business.

In my life, my father had gone bankrupt several times, had been visionary in his thinking but failed to operate a successful business on his own. Once my mother and my sister worked with him on one business he owned, and that business went way beyond anyone's expectations: phenomenal growth and financial success quickly and easily. This business was so successful because he could be the visionary and my mother and sister could organize, execute, market and sell. On his own, he couldn't implement the details necessary for success. Working together, as a crack team, they soared.

When I finally realized that I was "practicing being my father," my stomach and heart sank. I was devasted at who I was being. I hadn't gone so far as to be bankrupt, but I was acting in ways that I knew were counterproductive and ruining my chances for success. How could I practice being like my dad in business when he was a *disaster* in business in so many ways? But the truth of it was like a waking nightmare. Horrifying, but true.

One of the many key shifts in me came through the Eidetic Running for the Purpose of Making Money Image. (Try it for yourself here: www.WendyYellen.com/DTMBook). Another tectonic shift came when I came face to face with my inability to let go of my identification with my father's work inadequacies. It felt horrifying, and very real. My blinders were *finally* off. Instead of insisting on following him down his path of destruction, I began actually *doing and enjoying* what I needed and wanted to do for my business. It was interesting to watch myself repeatedly and easily saying *yes* instead of *no*. I could feel the old *no* in me briefly and then I could feel the *yes* come up instead. Weird but wonderful!

Being able to say *yes* to opportunities, people and helpful business practices allowed me to expand my practice, uplevel my presence online, and be much more visible. I was able to let go of staff who no longer served me and instead hire brilliant people who took care of me and my business at the highest levels. It was exciting for me to observe that my Achilles' heel of acting like my father was shifting faster and faster. I noticed, stopped, and reversed course more easily and with no drama.

Experiential exercise: (Running Image) Go here for a fascinating look at your natural energy and obstacles to that energy. www.WendyYellen.com/DTMBook.

Of course, parental identifications don't just affect our professional lives and results. Despite negative parental identifications, my client Kathryn created a brilliant career. Most of us would agree that when you love what you do, and you excel at it, when you are creative, passionate and energized by it, and others recognize you and seek you out, you've made it, right? Not Kathryn.

My client Kathryn is a brilliant, highly regarded fashion designer in her late 40s. Yet her disbelief in her own abilities left her feeling like a fraud, disowning her natural brilliance, feeling shame, and searching for other careers since she didn't feel good enough in her obvious choice. While disowning her passion, she dampened all of her enthusiasm for life through addictive behaviors and unsatisfying demeaning friendships.

One thing Kathryn claimed, repeatedly, was that she had a wonderful childhood. She held to this story despite her parents' verbal abuse of one another, drug use, lack of affection toward her, constant criticism and outright dismissal of her unique design talent and interest in fashion throughout her childhood. In some ways, it wasn't important for her to acknowledge these aspects of her childhood to herself just in and of themselves (although facing them helped her to navigate similar situations in her own life with more clarity). It was the insidious quality of her "insistent blindness" to the obstacles she threw in her own path that most impacted her life. She dabbled in drug use herself which often cost her to lose lucrative assignments. Her harsh judgments of others kept potential friends at arms' length. She was unconsciously verbally abusive to assistants, creating havoc and much turnover in her firm. She continually doubted her own talent which caused her to feel stress rather than joy in her work. She chose friends who were highly critical and who also felt unworthy of their success.

Kathryn's life was a riveting, astonishing denial of the incredible talent every other person saw in her but which she could not see. Not at all. Her insistent blindness to her abilities and her self-erected barriers was a tragedy, and she held onto that blindness every way she could, allowing its poison to seep into other areas of her life. Another part of her desperately wanted to get out from under herself. This willingness catapulted her into other *real* possibilities even though she tried to defeat herself, each step of the way.

I remember sitting with Kathryn in an adobe casita in Santa Fe to take her through her private day-long intensive. When Kathryn was introduced through an Eidetic image to a resource that was *already* part of her, she resisted *experiencing the feeling that was pulsating inside of her, even though she was starving to have it, and she resisted as if* her life depended upon it. The specific Eidetic exercise I used connects you to parts of you that have been buried deep inside by difficult parts of your history, including traumas at home, at school and in your culture. Most of us don't know how hard we fight against feeling good. Most of us don't recognize all the ways we defeat ourselves, because they feel automatic.

Kathryn recognized just how different she was feeling as she worked with the DTM process through her Eidetic images. She committed herself to this work with the same passion she used for her fashion design. Layer after layer of insistent blindness and long-held traumas fell off. Her creations now have even more panache, more daring. She feels confident enough to resist accepted runway trends and by doing so has attracted a customer base of loyal, raving fans who beg her for more. She's no longer shy about who she is, and she expresses it with a flair and energy that delights her.

Does Kathryn still have an inkling of self-doubt now and then? Yes, but it doesn't debilitate her. Can she occasionally still be harsh and cold to others? Yes, but she recognizes it and, because the stranglehold of her childhood traumas has alchemized to her kinder, more generous self, she is more likely to express warmth and understanding. Kathryn is still human. Yet now she more automatically and more effortlessly chooses the life-affirming options available from within her.

Filters

You've heard of looking at the world through rose-colored glasses so that everything seems, well, rosy. Filters are like looking through a kaleidoscope created by a trickster. What you see is a total distortion of the pieces used within the kaleidoscope. Yet you would swear that what you see is real and valid.

The filters we have in our mind control what we see, feel and experience in life. The filters that affect us the most are created by our experiences with our parents and often grandparents. Even parents who left your life early or were barely there also create a filter in you. Filters appear in every important aspect of life, and we all have *many*. For example, you have filters operating in you which control what you say to yourself (and the tone with which you say it!), how hard or easy or stressful it feels to have work success, how you even *define* success, the quality of love you can receive and give, how uncomfortable or safe you feel with other people, how you take care of your health, whether you are productive and effective or feel like you are frittering your life away, how you perceive yourself and others, how confident you feel, whether you apply yourself to a task with strain and tension or ease, how you interpret the events in your life, and everything else in the human experience. These filters, created by early experiences, are subtle and live inside you, quietly but relentlessly shaping the clay of your human existence. It could be an experience that stands out in your memory of your history, frequently occurring incidents or parental ways of handling life, or you may not remember specific incidents at all. But what we see and feel in ourselves and others who are important to us makes an impact on us and creates the glasses—rose-colored or trickster-designed—that you wear.

These filters can be positive or negative. Unfortunately, the negative ones, especially when we are unaware of them, heavily weigh us down, controlling what we perceive and therefore how we act and react to the world. Negative filters seem to naturally overwhelm our positive filters, but that can be changed.

For example, my mother's tightness and perfectionism made me feel distant from her as a child. But she also had other lovely qualities—softness, a wondrous sense of beauty, highly organized in a very professional way, and more. As a child, I didn't feel close to her partly because when her perfectionism came out, it came out against me. So, I distanced myself from *all* of her, and I could feel her distance from me. Unfortunately, this created in me a distance from *all* her qualities, including her organizational abilities, ability to create beauty, and more.

I worked very hard to overcome this negative parental filter because there was so much to gain from reconnecting to my mother (though she passed away decades ago). Not only am I able to embrace those qualities in me which had been dormant because of the negative filter, I also now have the gift of feeling her warmth,

> *"By repressing or trying to control what is repeatedly emerging from your depths, you create a barrier to accessing what is <u>underneath</u> what you are wanting to repress."*

kindness, tenderness and love, all of which were there before but which I couldn't feel. I carry that in me now.

Human nature being what it is, we often practice being like the more negative parent and perversely run away from the qualities of the more positive parent when, of course, those are what we need the most.

Reminder: These parental positive qualities are now inside of you, whether easily accessible or buried. Your parents probably both had some wonderful qualities, which are now in you in some way. If you are having trouble with this concept, or can't perceive those qualities in yourself, understand that your parents also had *their history*, and the crust of their history hid their positive qualities from themselves and from you.

But though hidden, everyone's resources remain inside within their little-used neural pathways. You, as a small child, sensed these resources even if they weren't apparent. All children feel the underlying healthy places in their parents. As a small girl I was positive that if I could just demonstrate to my mother the danger of smoking cigarettes, she would stop. I sensed that there was a hidden part inside her that wanted to be healthy and vibrant, even if she couldn't get herself to actually stop. And, eventually, she did.

To become our authentic selves, we need release from the control of these negative filters. It's not possible to be who you are when the shackles of your history control your every move. The Deep Transformation Method™ eases these negative filters that are thwarting your best intentions and brings the positive ones forward to support you. Now you can breathe.

Filters are not simply thoughts that you can toss away once you understand them. You can completely understand that you have a negative filter such as "I'm not worthy," "People can't be trusted", or "Life is a struggle," and even know intellectually that it is not true—yet it will still persist. You can do your best to get rid of it by attempting to repress or control it. But when you do that, you lose so much of yourself and your possibilities. By repressing or trying to control what is repeatedly emerging from your depths, you create a barrier to accessing what is *underneath* what you are wanting to repress. These aspects of yourself are there and waiting for you, including your natural ability to soften to love, delight yourself with your own creativity, experience ease in your approach to life and its obstacles, have more energy for what you want to do and feel an uprising of confidence when you step outside your comfort zone.

An example is my client Brian who thought he could control his anger towards his wife as his way to improve the way he acted towards her. But exerting control, while it avoided his unwanted angry outbursts, didn't make him open his heart or feel more loving. And that troubled him.

His filters were creating expectations, judgment and anger towards her. Which meant that, even though his wife was an intelligent, caring wife and mother and together they had created a life they both loved, he couldn't truly enjoy her fully because his filters were *distorting* his perception of who she was. He couldn't experience her *as she was*, only the much smaller woman that was colored by his filters.

He knew he didn't want to inflict a torrent of anger at his wife. He didn't want to be that kind of man. But though he could *control expressing* his anger using tremendous effort, he couldn't *open* himself to her. It's impossible to *force* openness in the heart. "You can't make your heart feel something it won't."

He had unconsciously learned these destructive patterns as a young child. His parents hadn't been able to be open and tender with each other. From inside their own burdened and hardened places, they had thrown critical barbs at him, disguised as compliments. This confused him as a young boy. In order to feel safe, he naturally protected his heart from them—from both the good and the bad. His parental filters slammed his heart shut. He equated marriage and relationships with pain and anger. He carried that filter and his wounded and shut heart into his marriage, leaving him feeling angry at someone who didn't deserve it, and feeling closed when he wanted to feel open. Brian's negative filters robbed him of much of the love he could give and receive.

Filters can also affect your success in your work. Say you have a favorite and beloved grandmother, Bubbie, who came over from the old country and whose formal education didn't go beyond high school. You might think that her history would disqualify her from exemplifying a positive filter for work success. She didn't have much education. She never ran a business and she doesn't know anything about business. But dismissing her would be a real loss.

Why? Because this Bubbie actually had a strong belief in the goodness of people and an excellent instinct for whom she could trust. She believed each person deserved respect and kindness and she showed it in a way that created loyalty in everyone she encountered. She believed that anything worth doing was worth doing well and knew that what she did mattered in the world. So, she gave lots of energy to projects that interested her and expressed a natural enthusiasm that inspired others to pitch in, whether it was for a fundraising bake sale or planting flowers at the local elementary school. She saw herself as having an innate ability to organize others which became evident every year when her Brownie troop sold more cookies than any other troop in the region!

You can see how Bubbie's filters would serve anyone well in business. Her *knowledge* about business might be lacking. But she shares many highly desirable traits, skills, and perceptions about life that are common in the most successful entrepreneurs.

But her son, your father, didn't take after his mother. He didn't value work, never enjoyed his job and didn't see any reason to improve at what he did. To him, work was just a place to show up from nine-to-five so he could pay the rent. He thought most people were naturally slackers, and he often complained about his co-workers. He was sure that his bosses were simply out to take advantage of him. His abrasive attitude made him unpopular and limited his advancement on the job. When not at work, he spent the majority of his time and energy fishing with his buddies.

However, you absolutely don't want a nine-to-five life for yourself. You have started to build a business that excites you. Yet, you have trouble building the team you need to truly make it successful. You hire good people yet their work product is lacking. Despite paying people well, you have a lot of staff turnover which costs you money and time. You feel that your contractors take advantage of you and you don't know whom to trust.

What if, instead of unconsciously using your father's filters in the workplace you could harness some of Bubbie's view of the world that gave her energy, organization, and talent at working with people? What if, instead of feeling let down or taken advantage of by others, you knew you could inspire them to excel? How could using different filters affect your business?

You *can* access Bubbie's abilities by easing the negative parts of your father filter (whose footsteps you are unconsciously following) and instead activating more of Bubbie's positive filters inside you. Notice how this is a two-step process. When one set of filters is negative and predominantly influencing you, we need to soften that influence. You also need and want access inside you to all of Bubbie's abilities. They make success so much easier and more fun.

It's important to both ease the iron grip of the negative filter and *also* to strengthen the ability of the positive filter to flow in.

There's another subtle but impactful aspect of filters. If you are someone who has energy and drive, you may want to be as different from your fishing-with-his-buddies father as possible. Understandably! But he may have *other* qualities that you would love to experience in yourself.

For example, what if, while he's fishing with his friends, your father tells stories and imparts wisdom to the other fishermen because he values friendship and sharing? What if he makes people laugh and feel good about themselves during these expeditions because he feels life should be appreciated and we are meant to uplift one another? His fishing expeditions are not only a fun, relaxing time but he's also giving his friends great memories and good advice-laced stories.

As the child of this man who loves fishing more than anything, you may only see the "laziness" and chafe against him. You don't admire him or feel proud of him. You don't really see or value his hanging out with his friends. You simply see him as lazy, not capable of being an entrepreneur like you want to be, and so you reject being like him. You believe you must act differently in every way or you won't be successful.

The result is that you unconsciously and automatically reject his positive filters and qualities at the same time. You disconnect from his light-heartedness, his calm, his gentle kindness and ease. Without easy access to this lightness, calm and ease, your success is stressed and strained. You feel the internal pressure to move, move, move, to be anything but lazy. Your body is tense, and you can't take your mind off work. You are now on track for burn-out because no one can reasonably and healthfully sustain a high-powered work life without also being able to access a calm, graceful, peaceful center.

It's difficult and *intense* to move from rejecting your "lazy" father to embracing his other qualities. Negative filters disconnect us from and deprive us of our rightful inheritance of our parents' positive qualities and filters. We think we have so many reasons to reject a parent, based on history. Of course, as far as we can see, we are right. The problem is that our filters keep us from seeing the whole picture. Our mind and the feelings in our body will fight madly to stay the same, to reject anything that might feel different but better, even though the fight against the self hurts so much.

"Who you think you are is the dust on your heart."

~ Krishna Das

Embracing something real, something new that goes against everything you have believed for decades, is *tough*. You must navigate new or less used neural pathways. The Grand Canyon pathways which we've used forever make us feel like we have no choice to act or think another way. One part of our mind fights, screams, bludgeons us, hurls daggers, begs us, blinds us in order to keep the old, deeply embedded ways. But this resistant part of the mind is not the deeper mind. When you contact your deeper mind, it feels expansive and true. When you act from that part of your mind, you *know* you are in the right place.

Stages of the Deep Transformation Method™

Deep transformation necessarily requires you to pass through and beyond your resistance to what you want, to your organic self. In order to pass through and beyond that resistance, and to embrace—truly *embrace*—who you are (even though it feels strange to feel good!), I've created my signature eight-stage Deep Transformation Method™ or DTM. This method, in fact, grew on its own as I observed what my clients and I needed to do, feel, and have in order to allow deep shifts to happen. The method I use is DTM, while the tool we use is Eidetics. These stages are not linear, and don't follow some prescribed sequence. Instead, they evolve naturally with each client's unique needs during their journey into relief and expansion. I think of these stages as part of an intricately woven braid, each contributing its part, and all necessary for transformation to be deep, real and lasting.

Stage One:
Harnessing Your Ability To Change: Neuroplasticity

As we've discussed, deep transformation requires a powerful tool and fortunately, you already have one in the innate neuroplasticity of the brain. While you may have heard of neuroplasticity, it's much more powerful and practical when you actually have the instruction manual. And giving you the owner's manual and having you *experience* different neuropathways in your own brain is the first step of the DTM method.

I didn't know Einstein and can't in any way say I know what he would think, or love. But I can *imagine* that going to this level of the psyche would be immensely entertaining and intriguing to his brilliant mind. He would recognize it as solving the problem on a different level.

Your private Grand Canyon hell feels like one foot on the gas, one foot on the brake, or taking two steps forward and three steps back. As a marketing copywriter, one of my clients constantly has looming client deadlines, graphic artists and formatters who urgently need her input, and frantic printers waiting for the finished files. But it takes five hours for her to do one hour of work because she spends hours responding to emails and texting and calling friends when she should be working. And she absolutely *can't stop herself or focus on what she knows she needs to do.* These delays, avoidances and distractions are versions of her own Grand Canyon.

If you've ever hiked out of the actual Grand Canyon, you know it's a wrench to leave because it's so beautiful. Even though you haven't seen a real toilet or shower for many days, and you've been sleeping rough, and the hike itself seems like such a daunting physical challenge. But once you start hiking up and out, you get the special treat of seeing the layers of the earth exposed on the canyon walls at eye-level as the earth rock gets younger and younger with each step up. You can see and even feel history in the rocks and layers as you hike out. You can't emerge from the Canyon without being immersed in the history of what has already occurred to the rocks and the plants and the water. Yet it's still hard work to get out.

It's a bit like that when you surface from your unique personal Grand Canyons. You've been down inside for decades, and so it feels familiar, like home. Often not very comfortable, but familiar. Part of you doesn't want to leave and doesn't believe you can. It feels oddly threatening to who you know yourself to be and who you think you are. You may not be in love with your limitations, but they feel very, *very* familiar.

I cannot over-describe the feeling of discomfort when you are offered a lifeline from your own psyche, but you feel yourself choosing pain and heartache instead. It happened with a client as I was editing this very chapter. She *knew* there was a way out, but she couldn't take it. Actually, she could, and did, and then didn't, and then did. The more she fought for her own limitations the more her Eidetic image gave her visceral gift after gift of the *experience* of being pulled out of the hole of her pain.

When you merely know intellectually that you can be different, it's real but not such an internal struggle. When you literally come face to face with your own brakes, feel yourself dig those heels into the ground and fight against the pull of freedom, now *that* is you grappling with yourself. It can be tiring. It can be exhilarating. It feels *very* real.

When you finally find a real way out, it's not easy because you can still feel the downward pull of history on you, even while you have your eyes on the top. Once you get out, there are all kinds of other beautiful canyons visible to explore, none of which you could see before. But they've been there all along.

Real transformation feels like that. And, just like the suddenly visible choice of other canyons, there are *always* other neural pathways already in you.

For Sara, who found reliable comfort and pleasure only in reading fiction, the urge to go down that books-for-comfort pathway was irresistible. As we worked to harness her powerful neuroplasticity for healing, she discovered her positive, lifegiving but hidden pathways. There *were* places in her history, people from her past, experiences she'd had that had laid positive pathways she could follow to find relief and connection and breathe more deeply.

For example, we found buried in her mind an old professor who had been kind to her, appreciated her work, and seemed to honestly like her. There was also a grandfather who had adored her and made her feel safe and cherished. *As remembered history*, these positive people in her life weren't able to erase the anguish or soften the pain in her current life. But through the Eidetic process and using the images as her starting point rather than regurgitating history, she was now able to *experience* the comfort and safety they brought to her, *in the present moment, not as fantasy but deeply in her mind and body*. Because these Eidetic images allowed her to *explore and experience* long buried neuropathways, she felt the experience fully in her body and emotionally. Sara became more accustomed to feeling safe, and her satisfaction organically grew as she tasted her immense talent for running a large non-profit, a talent she had had all along. She carried herself differently, and spontaneously proclaimed: "I feel pleased with myself." This is a statement she would have laughed at before she did the work to hike out of her Grand Canyon.[7]

When you are accustomed to unknowingly holding your breath in life, waiting for the other shoe to drop, expecting disaster around the corner or someone to desert you, you unconsciously undermine the positive of what is happening now. You tense up

7   Another fascinating part of Sara's work is that, as she was able to access positive parts of herself through these more peripheral filters in her life that were less threatening, she was also able to allow more of her parents' positive attributes to come through. This was something she had not been able to allow in at all before the locked door of her consciousness was pried open and the light began streaming through.

inside, knowing it won't—it can't!—last. How could it? It never has before.

In love, you may yearn, despite years of disappointment, to feel connection with your partner. When you look at your intimate partner and mentally go through your laundry list of complaints for the 100th time this week, rather than actually be with them in this moment and give your heart a chance to actually *feel* them, you are in a Grand Canyon of your relationship. Filters from your past color how much good you can let in, how much automatic criticism emerges from you, how much negativity you expect in relationships. Some of what happens between you and others comes from you, even though it can feel like it comes only from them. These filters obscure, even prevent, intimacy and connection.

When you are wrapped in your past, closed to whatever good is trying desperately to come through to you, your body and mind tighten against the positives in the present. Instead, you remain absolutely certain horrors are coming next.

You can't *explain* away the feeling of waiting for the other shoe to drop, because it's a Grand Canyon neural pathway. But, harnessing the power of neuroplasticity, we can find places already inside of you that actually *know* another way. It's just that those pathways are congested and less accessible from disuse.[8]

Once my clients begin to travel on a lesser used but shockingly positive and helpful neural pathway, they often point to their brain, a puzzled look on their face. "I feel like something is changing in my brain, like it's being rewired." This sensation of being rewired is one which many people have described when talking with me after an especially intense piece of discovering and experiencing unused neural pathways.

Another client, Michelle, a 40ish single mother corporate executive automatically created a protective wall around herself

8   Through the use of fMRI imagery, researchers are able to actually track the physical process that occurs in the brain when you start to travel down these pathways. https://www.ncbi.nlm.nih.gov/books/NBK538909/

in order to get through her day. She didn't feel welcome or even seen in the world. After one private session, Michelle said it felt weird to feel safe and protected. "Such a foreign feeling to feel happy and excited to see my parents, and that they are happy and excited to see me. Not what I would have expected."

Michelle was describing what becomes the fun part of accessing the ability to shift to a different, already present, pathway: You surprise yourself in delightful ways. And you delight yourself in surprising ways.

Instead of unconsciously or deliberately creating "protective" walls between you and others, you experience the *connection* between you. Your heart opens, you feel touched by what you have together, open to them in ways you didn't know you could experience. For example, the tension between you and your young adult daughter dissolves, not just inside *you*, but you can feel how open *she* is to you, how much she *wants* that closeness. You are so surprised—she didn't act this way before! Her changes, wonderful as they feel to you, don't make sense to you *logically*, since *you* are the one doing the work to change. But it *does* make sense because your new openness to yourself and to her *is affecting her even though she may not be able to articulate it or even consciously realize it.*

Christine is a lovely, quiet, deeply spiritual, high-powered professional in her early 50's who knows how to get things done. It shocked her when she began to discover something she had never understood about herself: she erects a brick wall between herself and others. Despite her intelligence and sensitivity, *she had no idea.* Other people, however, had been feeling it all along, and subtly backed away from her as they unconsciously honored the message she sent out. Christine learned to build a wall to protect herself during multiple massive losses in her childhood. She needed this wall of seeming safety so she didn't get overwhelmed by the pain. As these creations go, the wall did its job, but also had unintended effects.

She felt removed enough from others to feel safe, but she was also now removed from *herself.* She felt a bit numb. And this numbness enhanced the feeling of aloofness that others experienced with her—an aloofness which she absolutely did *not* feel towards others. In fact, just the opposite.

Contacting her deeper feelings was something Christine had stayed away from as a child, because it wasn't safe. Through the DTM process and as she eidetically experienced new neural pathways, she began to experience the world as safe, and the wall was no longer needed. She didn't need to smash it or disassemble it. She didn't talk to it and tell it to go. She didn't try to live without it. *None of those more logical, self-directed, solving-the-problem-on-the-level-at-which-it-was-created solutions were enough.*

Instead, the wall softened on its own as she experienced, deep in her body, that she was safe. No directives were needed for her to stop pushing people away, or for her to create boundaries instead of walls, or anything else that didn't come from the beautiful center of her which had already existed but had been hidden away.

Some of my clients explain these kind of changes as new levels of vibration. Some talk about it as their heart chakra opening. For me, I appreciate the neuroscience of it, and am awed by the beauty. But whatever way you perceive it, this is what predictably happens when you do the real work of DTM.

Experience for Yourself: Exploring an Old Neuropathway

Name three situations that you fear the worst, where you can't imagine it'll come out okay. Think about health, aging, intimate loves, work or your business.

Now pick one of those situations, and do your best to find out what you have held yourself back from because you feared the worst or were waiting for the other shoe to drop. Examples might be: You didn't love a certain person because you were afraid to lose them. You didn't contact that colleague you wanted to connect with because you thought they wouldn't receive you well. You thought about that trip but worried about going alone.

Describe for yourself what you notice in your body and in your thoughts as you go through these questions. Look for places of tension, for thoughts of wanting to get away from your experience of yourself. Perhaps you are shaking your head because you recognized that you were avoiding doing something that could be beneficial but you still did it—and you still do it! This is the power of a well-traveled neuropathway. The good news is that once you have cleared and strengthened new, positive neuropathways, they will have that same power.

Stage Two:
Softening and Releasing Traumas and History

"Trauma and painful history create a choke hold on your body, literally stiffening, hardening, and limiting you physically, emotionally, mentally, and even spiritually."

All along the journey, the Deep Transformation Method™ and all of Eidetic imagery work harness the genius of neuroplasticity to support deep change. To achieve lasting change in the parts of your life that make a difference to you, it's *also* essential to soften and release traumas and painful history. We all have traumas, big and small. Trauma and painful history create a choke hold on your body, literally stiffening, hardening, and limiting you physically, emotionally, mentally, and even spiritually.

It can feel daunting to think about your history and even more scary to consider revisiting traumas that already have hurt you more than you care to remember.

Dealing with trauma does NOT need to be what you may think it is. When my clients deal with traumas, even during the very first pass, they are stunned at how relieved they feel and how much more they feel like who they really are. This is a different way of working with trauma and history that does not feel like regurgitating your whole life and does not feel like you have to relive the trauma. Far from it.

It isn't fantasy or positive thinking, neither of which, in my experience, are strong enough to allow a woman to re-emerge with her trauma-buried resources intact and flourishing. Before I explain why this is so, let's look at what happens when the crust of your history, with its layers of all your traumas, still has a stranglehold on you.

Ann's father abandoned the family when she was very young. She barely remembers him, and her mother never spoke of him. Her mother had grown up at a time when the man of the household was the breadwinner. Yet she was now burdened with raising the family alone. Although Ann's mother was able to create a very lucrative career, she missed not being taken care of by the man who had left her. Ann grew up witnessing a stressed and overworked mother, and felt it was her job to take care of her mother.

Now forty, Ann also has an excellent, well-paying job for which she has great passion and skill. She has lived as an independent, successful woman for many years. Yet in a secret corner of her independent heart, she longs for a man to take care of her. She also pushes men away because she "knows" they will abandon her, just as her father abandoned her mother. To avoid being devastatingly hurt again, she leaves them before they can leave her first. Even (or perhaps, especially) the ones she loves most.

There are layers upon layers of her history imprisoning Ann and creating aspects of her that are not her organic, original self.

Ann fears repeating that devastating feeling of the loss of her father, so she avoids closeness with men, while at the same time searching and longing for that closeness. She can't win against herself, because whether she gets close to a man or leaves him, the need which is not being fulfilled (either safe independence or closeness) surfaces to make her miserable. She is fiercely independent, yet she yearns to be taken care of. She can't go fully in either direction because the opposite desire defeats her.

Ann still feels responsibility for her mother's burdens, which results in her both loving and resenting her mother. She can't feel too close, and she can't shake off the guilt.

In conversation, in relationship, in life, Ann wants to get to the point of things quickly and move on. When she does this, she thinks it's just her way to process the world, and even likes it. From the outside, though, it feels subtly but rudely dismissive and impatient, even superficial. And it helps explain why she has trouble having close women friends.

This quickness, which modern culture celebrates, has a dark underbelly for Ann. It disguises the discomfort that has been brewing inside of her since she was small. When she is quick and dismissive, she doesn't have to *feel*. Feeling is uncomfortable because it uncovers hidden painful feelings and takes her back to the loss of her father and the difficult years she witnessed in her mother's life. This translates into a staccato feeling in her life, a rapid-fire skimming of the surface despite her spoken desire to be more connected to her heart. She has contradictory feelings and desires, and the impatient part wins out, much to the sorrow of her heart.

All of this is largely unconscious, which means that it runs the show inside of her, controlling how she experiences the world, tightening her body, and creating barricades to connection which are wholly unrecognized, yet deeply painful.

For Ann to be gracefully unleashed, she needed to experience the part of her that was *still* trying to take care of her mother, rather than being run by that part unconsciously. Part of the difficulty for Ann was the *way* she felt involved with her mother—anxious, worried, angry, a bit resentful, and unable to extricate herself and feel her own needs. As she was gradually willing to go back and actually *feel* the part of her that was so worried for her mother, paradoxically it unleashed her from that worry. Not just from the worry for her mother but worry about caring for people in general (and then resenting it when she did). When something in us drives us unconsciously, it can be painful and quite difficult to feel it, but when we are willing to be *in* the soup of our life, rather than removed from it, life looks different. What we didn't want to feel is no longer dragging us around by the scruff of our neck.

In a very short time, Ann began to feel more comfortable being with men she was meeting, less self-critical and less guarded. However, she remained unaware of the ways she was subtly dismissive of others and the way her over-quick analysis was keeping her disconnected from herself and from others. This was not an area she wanted to delve into, and it would have been difficult work for her. That level of work is not for everyone. She was satisfied with her success from our brief work together, which was freedom to feel like herself with men, and to feel less guarded about meeting new potential partners. I did feel sad that she stopped when she did, because I have a real sense of just how free and expansive a person can feel once they dive deep and grapple with these more invisible places.

Another client, Laurie, is a 55+ marathon runner who owns her own hand-made paper products business, one that overflows with her creative, kind energy. People see her products and can't wait to surround themselves with her creations. Yoga, meditation, art and music are her passions.

The crust of Laurie's history was crushing her when we met. I couldn't help being drawn to her despite the quiet cloud of anxiety that surrounded her. This dark cloud furrowed her brow and burdened her shoulders but somehow her light still eked through. I was so glad when she decided to do this work with me. I *knew* she could feel differently, and on some level, so did she.

Laurie's father physically and emotionally abused her mother, herself and her younger sister. He dishonored the family's trust in multiple ways but held power over everyone and no one was able to escape emotionally or physically. Mother cowered, younger sister carried it silently, and Laurie felt responsible and tried to make it all okay for everyone. She was taking on an impossible task.

The family put on a smile for the outside world, while inside they trembled, each alone in their own room, with their own fear, for decades.

Today Laurie's sister is in and out of various institutions, struggling with addictions and attracting abusive relationships with men and women. Laurie took on the responsible child role, which served her well but also injured her.

This is the way with our wounds. We develop enormous capacities to cope and survive. But the *way* that we have learned to survive creates painful vulnerability and unfortunate coping strategies which become our Achilles' heel. Laurie's way of getting through life—over-responsibility—created her need to try to help people who (like her parents) didn't want to accept or weren't able to accept any help, including hers. Doing this came at a steep price. She almost lost her business because of the time she spent trying to rescue others, and she came close to legal troubles which in fact had nothing to do with her, but that could have cost her everything.

None of this should have happened to Laurie. Who she was and is at her core is a kind, caring, responsible, beauty-loving woman. But her history had twisted those parts of her so they now worked against her. We really had to make a difference soon, because these patterns were getting worse and making more and more trouble for her.

They were also aging her.

In an earlier chapter, we talked about negative identification with a parent. The trauma of Laurie's early life led to negative parental identification with *both of her parents*. Prying loose that negative identification with both of her parents was what saved Laurie from her own self-destruct button.

When you are bent on self-destruction, even though you don't really see it that way, odds are there is a negative identification or filter going on with one or both parents. Laurie had one with both her father and her mother. I also had both when I began working with Dr. Ahsen. Some people have just one.

But when a parent is abusive, emotionally absent, drinking too much, judgmental, harsh or otherwise negative, and their tenderness and love are difficult to feel, then what *you* take in, unconsciously, is *their* negative qualities and they become *your* negative parental filter. Because you were afraid of them or distanced yourself from them as a child to protect yourself, you also, again unconsciously, rejected the parts of your parent which were positive and which could have helped you.

In Laurie's case, after retrieving many powerful, independent aspects of her that had been buried (but had been patiently waiting) beneath the traumas of her childhood, we then worked with her filters. For Laurie, *both parental filters were negative.* In her history, neither one supported her, neither one saw her. Because these negative behaviors created a template in Laurie, a filter, she unconsciously re-created what she had experienced as a child in her adult relationships. Laurie felt a need to save others, to inflict self-abuse within relationships, and felt a constant underlying hum of anxiety and tension in her body along with a feeling that she wasn't loved.

What does gracefully unleashed look like in Laurie? Awareness was the *first* key for Laurie. Consistently being conscious of the filters so she isn't operating with her eyes closed to what she is doing to herself. She could no longer act out her old patterns because now she naturally and instantly *felt* the effect on herself of what she was doing. It stopped her in her tracks.

Once she could no longer blindly harm herself emotionally, what emerged was a night-and-day difference. Laurie incorporated self-care into her life, taking time for herself, and following the passions she had long ago let drift away but now felt anew. She experienced an ease in her brow and shoulders so that old aches and pains softly released. She told me she needed far fewer medical appointments, massages and chiropractic work to get her through her week. She acted and felt younger and more vibrant, something others consistently noticed in her.

I once worked with a talented father of three, a psychologist, whose father had died young of a debilitating degenerative illness. We worked deeply with how the image of his father's physical degeneration had dampened their connection. One memory image he had with his father was of swimming together in the evening in the family pool. He had wonderful memories of this time before his father got sick. But that was when he was very young. As he got older, his father's physical deterioration devasted him.

The trauma of watching his father disintegrate before his eyes started to play out in his own life. He often felt unwell and lacked energy though he was only in his early 40s. He described himself as "aging quickly" and felt he was "fading fast." He spent time ruminating about dying though he had no obvious diagnosis that said his death was imminent.

In his Eidetic images he spontaneously saw the two of them swimming together when he was a young adult. This felt like a real experience and gave him enormous pleasure as he felt very connected to this vibrant, alive father. As a young man, seeing his father degenerate sapped him of his own energy as a youth. But seeing his father energetic and powerful created a feeling of well-being inside him *now* which was very real and which he felt in his body and especially in his heart. In a wonderful example of how deeply this changed him, he told me years later that when people asked him about his father, the father he now remembers is the father swimming laps alongside him in his late teens. He feels this strong, invigorating father in his cells, and he feels that strength inside himself. That's how strongly and deeply the images transformed him.

Experience for Yourself: How Old Trauma May be Affecting You Now

This exercise is similar to one I've used with my Eidetic Mastermind, after which we worked on what came up for each person. I strongly suggest that you go through this exercise ONLY when you feel in a good, strong space inside yourself to touch on your traumas. Don't do it if you feel you don't have good support right now. You don't want to re-traumatize yourself especially if you would have to deal with it by yourself (which is most likely how you had to deal with it when it happened). If you don't have good support, simply skip over this exercise for now.

Here's the exercise: Pick one of your most constant concerns or feelings in life (even if you don't always feel/believe those concerns are justified). It should be one that comes up regularly especially when you feel down, like: "I don't matter." "No one really cares about me." "I always try to notice and recognize people, but no one does that for me." "I have no real talent." "I don't deserve XYZ." "This problem will never get better." Pick one or more that are your "go-to" feelings and are with you regularly. They sneak in when you're tired, disappointed, defeated, etc. Write them down. We'll call these your default mode. It's not always there but it's lurking in the background. Now go through your history in your mind and write down traumas—single events or events that occurred regularly, especially when you were growing up. You can also include more recent ones. Write them down.

Now for each trauma, write beside it what feeling you have about yourself when you go back in your mind to the trauma. Not the intellectual thought about it, but the feeling you still have even though you may have "worked" on it. Go below the surface to answer.

Now look at the feelings from the traumas, and your default mode feelings when you feel down or depressed. What patterns do you see? What do you understand about how these early traumas might be affecting the way you see the world? Try to go deeper and be very honest with yourself, so you can learn more than you already know.

Stage Three:
Uncover What is Already Inside You

"The emptiness of the gap is filled by the leap."

~ *Akhter Ahsen*

When you harness the power of neuroplasticity and soften and release traumas and resistance to yourself, what emerges is massive relief. You experience the resources and abilities inside you which you had forgotten, disconnected from, or, sadly, had given up on completely. The various stages of the journey support each other and create the rewiring that so many of my clients comment on.

One woman uncovered the gifted writer she really is. More importantly, she embraced that part of herself and took off flying as an author. The release and the pleasure in her author-self made her giddy with relief, pleasure and joy.

Another woman, Elaine, a mother and professional in her 40s, who had suffered emotional abuse in her every waking moment as a child, had hardened her heart against the world, understandably so. Her long road back to herself began and she uncovered a new feeling: the ability to empathize with her twelve year-old son and her life-partner Audrey. The hard heartedness of her single-parent father made it very difficult for Elaine to contact anyone with anything even remotely like understanding or empathy, including herself. But once she was able to experience pain, hers or someone else's, *without being overwhelmed by it*, she no longer pushed away her son or her partner, and both automatically and naturally drew closer to her. This was Elaine, becoming gracefully unleashed.

Most of the people I work with don't actually know what is inside of them. They don't deeply grasp the resources and qualities they already possess. These people are intelligent, thoughtful people of integrity who are familiar with self-reflection and have worked on themselves in various ways. How, then, is it possible that they don't know who they are? That they don't know their true essence and can't take in what is so obviously true of their deep nature? And is it truly possible to discover and appreciate your value, even into your 40's, 50's and beyond?

Yes.

Most of my clients are already in their 40's or older when they find me, and most have that question. Here are a few more quick examples of people who thought they were too old to really change and then uncovered magnificent potential in themselves after working with me:

The 60+ year old husband and father who spontaneously asked his wife out on a date for the first time in their decades-long marriage.

The 42 year-old woman who went hang-gliding after years of terror of heights and of fear of being seen in public.

The 45 year-old father, extreme sports enthusiast and business owner (who suffered a mind-numbing fear of heights and flying after almost driving off an icy bridge) who sent me a video of himself grinning as he threw himself boldly off the platform bungy jumping.

The mother whose heart felt torn from her chest because of the estrangement with her teenage son, who healed their relationship so much that *he* now sends her loving texts out of the blue.

The 52 year-old artist who felt ashamed of calling herself an artist who now displays her art proudly and has people clamoring for her work.

The 55 year-old woman who couldn't love her husband because he was A, B, and C instead of X, Y, and Z, but who found a way to actually know *him* from a real part of *her* and was able to die peacefully with him lovingly beside her every step of the way.

The 48 year-old business owner who stepped into her business fully, giving it the attention and energy that it—and she—deserved.

The 45 year-old successful and published writer who felt like she was "going to her own execution" every time she sat down to write who was finally freed up and at ease in her writing, simply getting down to business and writing.

The 62 year-old business owner who wanted to crawl under his desk and hide for weeks when a promotion went south who instead rapidly and gracefully turned the whole event into one of his biggest marketing successes.

Who knows what is inside you waiting to come out? It could be love, confidence, strategies for success, ways to gracefully implement with less stress, thoughtfulness, courage, adventure, curiosity, stellar abilities and big grins.

Yes, *real change* is possible, whether you are 42 or 62 (or 82!). It's not too late to bring forward what is inside you. The earlier you start, the more years you have to embrace more and more of the essential you, you without the shackles of your history weighing you down and dragging along with you.

What is it like to uncover what is inside you? What do you imagine it feels like to be yourself? First, do you even have a sense of who that could be? You most likely have a partial sense. But your sense of yourself is colored and minimized by early experiences, which means you can't really take in all of your abilities and resources and qualities. How could you when so much of you is buried beneath that crust of history? This happens to *all* of us.

Even a highly successful business owner can *still* be shackled by their history. You can be successful and still not be uncovering all that is inside of you that could make your success easier, more graceful and, yes, happier. There are different ways to become successful, and when success includes excessive *internal* stress and angst and consistent *repetitive* problems, there is probably more of you available as a helpful resource that you aren't tapping. All businesses have to deal with problems, but it's the way you feel and the way you think about them that makes the difference in your quality of life. This is true whether you are the business owner, the team leader, or a team player.

One super successful lawyer I worked with could have had even greater success, with a lot less drama and staff problems, much earlier. He was hampered because he was practicing being like his father. He had been brought up by his mother as if he could do no wrong and by a father who would never listen to anyone, including my client. This meant that he felt he could be less than thoughtful about the way he handled clients, and they wouldn't mind. It also meant that he had a deaf ear to any helpful input just like his father. These were extremely difficult identifications to release because he was so successful on the one hand, yet he was (blindly) dragging himself down on the other. Fortunately, he was eager, and very willing, to shift these parts of himself.

For him, uncovering what was already inside him meant finding the caring man who actually *did* put others needs and wants into the mix, not just his own needs. This change made a longed for and loving difference with his wife and adult children and made him much happier. These more thoughtful aspects of him had been well buried. When we first started working together, he didn't know that his more self-centered way of viewing the world was actually standing solidly in the way of even greater ease, love and success. As that changed, he became much more easygoing, and an even more successful husband, business owner and father.

What is the *experience* like when you uncover what is inside you? It's not as straightforward as you might imagine. Change is challenging, even change that we *want*. The process of uncovering your resources and organic wholeness, along with the experience of uncovering yourself through eidetic images, a visceral invitation to be more of yourself. You can feel what you are holding back and you feel what is available, all at once. There really isn't a need to make a choice. When you stay with Eidetic experience, the images themselves blaze the trail through those old neural pathways, clearing the way and inviting you inexorably forward. You don't have to *do* anything-except stay with the process. And that brings us to the next stage, experiencing your resources.

Experience for Yourself: What IS inside you?

I want to *show* you this part of yourself. Go here for a short experiential video to give you a lovely glimpse of what is still inside you, ready and waiting to come out! www.WendyYellen.com/DTMBook.

Stage Four:
Experience Your Resources
(Even on a Bad Hair Day)

Once you have traveled more often down those positive neural pathways that you have inside you and feel supported after dissolving the hold that history and trauma have on your peace of mind, and you have uncovered what is already inside of you, the next step in DTM is to *experience* those resources more fully. To have them become as familiar as your breath, natural and easily accessible. We go beyond intellectual understanding and into a full-body *knowing* that bursts right through any bad hair day—as well as any stressors that throw you *way* off track more than any bad hair day could.

You go from massive amounts of despair and self-loathing to spontaneously and unexpectedly feeling pleased about yourself.

You go from rejecting your passions and skills to wanting your grandchild to remember you as a creative.

You stop fighting against dull but necessary exercise and join a Pickleball team, where you sweat, meet fun people, and can't wait to get there.

You shock yourself by saying "yes" to your partner—and it feels so easy! The light in their eyes and the smile on their face makes you want to do it again and again.

The part of you that needs to be right and craves to be perfect has left the building and you are open to exploring, experimenting, and even looking inept while trying something new. (Okay, maybe not entirely left the building but there's a lot of space between you and her.) What a relief!

At work, you accomplish feats of organization, team management, task completion and easy focus that were elusive before. You aren't forcing this on yourself or anyone. You aren't whipping yourself into a frenzy. Instead, the curious, interested, even playful aspects of you come naturally to the fore. You're stunned.

Each of these are specific examples of women just like you, as they worked their way through the Deep Transformation Method™ and began to experience their resources.

When we feel fear, our mind tightens. We batten down the hatches to prepare for disaster, so ideas have trouble coming in. Our mind races and thus we risk rejecting good ideas that could help, all of which means we are solving problems with less than all of our creative intelligence and abilities. You know what this feels like. It's hard to have the patience to *listen* even to ideas that could help. You're tempted to cut corners to go faster, which only creates more problems.

Here's a great example from a *New York Times* best-selling author:

"After a colleague told me about the fast and astonishing results he got with DTM and Eidetics, I got jealous. I wanted to see what it could do for me. One of the things that I particularly wanted help with was I had been feeling really stuck on some of the marketing projects I had wanted to implement. I just couldn't seem to sit down and put pen to paper, to write the marketing pieces that I needed to write. It had been going on for months. It was really frustrating me and weighing down on me.

After Wendy took me through a specific Eidetic image, I experienced an immediate breakthrough. The next day, I wrote a marketing piece in one hour, that was nearly in final form in one draft. Normally, something like that would take me at least four to eight hours.

During Session Two, I got a very <u>different</u> image that enabled me to have an even bigger breakthrough on another marketing piece I needed to create. This time, I wrote it in less than 30 minutes AND something happened that has NEVER happened before. The piece was so good after the first draft, that I didn't want or need to change a single word (saving me 4-8 hours of _agony_!) The copy I had written fit the space I had _perfectly_! That's _never_ happened to me before either. I almost always write too much copy and then agonize for hours about what to cut out. The breakthroughs keep _building_ on themselves one after the other. It's become my secret weapon!"

Experience for Yourself: Who Are You Really?

When you were a child, you loved something about yourself. Maybe you loved that you read in bed hiding under the blanket with a flashlight. You sang out loud on your bicycle whenever you went fast. Your Pooh Bear was your best friend. Kitty slept on your chest and purred you to sleep every night, and you didn't move for fear of waking her. Perhaps you smile when you think about skipping stones in the creek bed near your grandparent's house or knowing that you made up wild suffragette stories about your eccentric aunt, or that when your parents were away, your solution to the suddenly leaking roof as a nine year-old was, obviously, to call a plumber. You have something like that, even when it's your secret.

Dig deep. Find one that makes you smile. What quality in you comes through? Imagination? Curiosity? Love for animals? A sense of adventure? That quality is still there. We just need to uncover it.

Stage Five:
Give Your Transformation a Boost

The way people typically go about dealing with a problem, and how DTM and Eidetics approach it, are fundamentally different. Once you master this simple yet profound shift in the way you move through your internal obstacles, it's easier to breathe. It's easier to feel your accomplishments. It's easier to deal with the inevitable problems of life. It's easier to be more of who you are. Why? Because you start from a more open, less reactive, part of you. You automatically feel like you have more choices, because you do. You are not locked into what you *already* think and feel. Doing something differently doesn't feel like an insurmountable or exhausting hurdle. It feels doable.

When you are accustomed to responding to life in certain specific ways—irritation at a spouse, impatience with a project, disappointment in yourself, thinking you should be better dealing with this kind of situation at your age—those familiar patterns easily emerge when difficulties or obstacles pop up. When you aren't locked into what you already have thought or felt, you experience a massive softening of the *resistance* you felt against change, new thoughts, or recognizing your less-than-enlightened ways. You find yourself naturally being with and feeling towards your partner in ways you wouldn't have thought possible before, trying new systems in your business, shifting your management style, or taking better care of your body.

As another client, Marcy, a 45-year-old mother and private school administrator, began her journey out of the depression and anger which had haunted her since she was a young woman, the first obstacle she had to face was that she had no idea what feeling *good* felt like. And when she began to experience feeling safe and calm and relaxed for the first time in decades, it felt "weird."

Of course it felt weird! We become so accustomed to feeling off, sad, confused, aggravated, angry and distant that any positive feelings are like an intruder. Who is that and how did they get here? Ironic, because of course this intruder is actually *your invited guest*. But so goes the contradictory way we humans are wired. Consistency isn't our strong suit. And we are *far* from logical.

Which is why *any process that works with the mind can't depend on what we think. Our conscious mind's main tool is logic, and we simply aren't logical.*

Starting the process of change by trying to think our way out of it, or feel our way out of it, doesn't feel weird. It feels familiar and somewhat comfortable. However, we can't think in a different way when we use our old ways of thinking to change our thinking. When we *start* the process from how we feel, we inadvertently introduce feelings *created during traumatic parts of our history* rather than reaching new or different aspects of ourselves. Familiar but not effective.

Starting the change process with an Eidetic image, instead of thinking or feeling or logic or repeating memories, gives transformation a powerful advantage and boost. It starts the change process with a part of our mind that is fresh, creative, inspired, organic, and naturally whole.

My client Marcy juggled a life of handling one burning hot potato after another, often six or seven scorching potatoes at one time. She can't move fast enough to keep ahead of things. She fights so many fires at once that putting out one barely lowers the blazing heat. What she deals with, between home, husband, kids and work, isn't actually possible for one woman. Yet that is exactly what she does. When she came to me, she wasn't at her wit's end. She had reached *that* place years before. And yet she still kept up with all the family needs and the huge demands of her work: a highly successful professional on the outside, stressed to the breaking point on the inside.

Marcy is thoughtful, self-reflective, intelligent and no stranger to therapy. We needed something powerful right away, to give her room to breathe.

After experimenting a bit to see which Eidetic image was best for *her*, and for this specific problem, I chose one of the dozens of images meant to lower the red-hot high alert of the mind so Marcy could think instead of react or be constantly overwhelmed.

Within minutes she began to visibly relax, breathe deeper, feel better, and think more clearly. "I feel more peaceful, cooled down, calmed down, and the whole problem feels more under control."

Immediately, the seemingly unresolvable but pressing decision she had brought up earlier clarified itself and the answer was obvious to her.

You can't think clearly when your mind is racing and you are running from one emergency to another. But once the mind relaxes, your natural intelligence asserts itself.

I *could* have tried to reason out the possibilities and options with her. Brainstorming and entertaining new ideas can be productive and eye-opening. But what I wanted for her, and for you, is to *experience* the difference when the high alert stress calms down inside and you can organically, naturally find your way to the right answer.

There was more than the one decision she needed to make. She needed—and craved—to find a state of deep connection with herself, beyond the heat of the moment and her life, to be able to think clearly and resolve creatively. She also needed to experience peacefulness and safety inside herself to do that. The problem she really needed to resolve went way beyond the question of "Shall I do A or B?" that had been presented as the immediate concern. To handle the real, underlying issue, Marcy needed the boost: the resources from her Eidetic level of consciousness.

Experience for Yourself: Cooling the Stress[9]

You can also access this experiential exercise in more depth here: www.WendyYellen.com/DTMBook.

Think about something that sets your hair on fire. Something that makes you want to scream or run away or pound your head on a wall. Think about it until you *feel* as stressed as you usually do when it's actually happening. Let the feelings exist in you as you think about it. Don't try to make them go away. Stay within the experience no matter how uncomfortable. You are simply contacting a place inside you that still feels this way underneath. If you can't get it to ignite right now, pick a different stressful issue or situation.

Now see your brain in an image. Look carefully at your brain. Look at the outside, then deep inside, including the crevices and hidden places. What is the temperature of your brain in your image? We're not interested in what you think it would or should be. Actually look at the brain and see what it *is in this moment.*

Wherever you find heat, including hidden heat, or red colors, *see* that you are pouring cold slushy ice on the heated places. You have all the cold slushy ice in the universe available to you. Continue to pour or shovel it on the hot places until you see the hot places cool to normal brain temperature. ALL of the places. Keep going until your brain is normal brain temperature.

Helpful Hint: You are NOT trying to calm yourself down. You are cooling down the brain. The goal is to cool the brain. If you are very stressed, it may take a loooooooong time. Keep at it.

Once the brain is normal brain temperature, or even just quite a bit cooler, notice how you feel, how your mind and thoughts and body feel. For almost everyone, icing the brain this way takes the pressure off in significant and helpful ways.

Rinse and repeat as often as needed. The more you do this

9 © 2009 Dr. Akhter Ahsen, PhD Private Intensive Session

Eidetic image, the more you can lower your set point of heat and create a new normal *which you will experience as more ease.*

This exercise is one example of giving your transformation a boost by not starting with thinking or feeling, but by going to another level of your mind. This approach also harnesses the genius of neuroplasticity and uncovers what is already inside you. I once did a similar image with a group of financial advisors and, of course, I did it myself as I walked them through it. We spent most of the group session on it. Deepening, deepening, deepening. This was the first time I did one of Ahsen's ice images for more than ten minutes or so. Since that day, of course, I still experience stress at times. But I don't go to the same level of stress and I can find relief much sooner. It still astonishes me that this level of shift is possible.

Stage Six:
Overcome Resistance to Change

Resistance can pop up at any stage in the journey. You may experience resistance even *entertaining* the thought of going beyond the layers of your history. You may feel resistance to sensations in your body that are unfamiliar and seem too wonderful to be true. And you may encounter resistance after experiencing the sometimes shocking resources of your Self. It's at this point in the DTM process that you decide whether to continue opening to those resources or keep repeating your disruptive but oddly comfortable patterns and filters.

When our history has trauma—and we all have trauma in life—we experience a not-safe, frightening sense of vulnerability. Those vulnerabilities make us feel especially sensitive and so we create a layer of overprotection to guard against more pain. Ironically, in order not to be overwhelmed by feeling too vulnerable, we create a shield around us, protecting us but also leaving us less flexible. As we become less flexible, we prefer the path we've gone down before, and shy away from anything new in an effort to protect ourselves from even more pain.

Our well-worn pathways may not even be our *own* way, but instead the way of one or both of our parents. They may be parental examples that we have come to firmly believe in. But we'll cling to them even when we consciously know they do not serve us. Those ways are now inside of us. We learn when we are young from repeated life experiences, even if no one says a word. It seeps in through our pores. We learn how to love and how to be unkind. We learn what is approved and what is frowned upon. We learn about how to handle money and how to handle adversity. We learn whether or not it's okay to feel good about yourself, or if it's okay to have abilities your brother doesn't have. We learn.

My father went bankrupt three times. I was terrified I "had his genes." His way with money exacerbated my mother's sense of shame about not being perfect. This highly skilled, kind, beautiful and gracious woman trembled and hid whenever a stranger knocked on the door, fearing that it was another legal notification against my father. Her shame was profound.

As I was expanding my psychotherapy practice from local to international, I was terrified that as I stepped into this larger arena, I would inadvertently follow him down that path of destruction. I already recognized the seeds within me. The terror about my own self-destruct button led me to Eidetics.

I had other, much-needed abilities in me too from both parents, but I had unconsciously rejected some of the ones I now needed the most. My job was to re-connect with my genetic abilities and disconnect from my father's self-destructive ways so that I would naturally steer clear of impending doom. I had a lot of work in front of me. But it felt like life and death, and it was *my* life, so I chose life.

Because I had strongly embedded self-destructive habits, I definitely had to grapple with myself, with my resistance to feeling better. I had to wrestle with the dangerous, hidden lethargy in me that was revealed during my personal eidetic sessions which threatened my ability to grow my business and make good business choices. Someone can offer you a lifeline, but you do need to grab onto it and use it, not just put it away for another day when it feels comfortable or convenient.

Through the Eidetic process, you get to repeatedly experience another way of being, another set of resources, a you who is more authentic and unleashed. Yet after having those experiences, you can still argue against yourself, or reject that freedom with your mind. In that way, it is still up to you to choose whether to continue in your old patterns or expand into this new level of yourself. And that shift can be frightening and uncomfortable at first. The old neuropathways still feel more comfortable and familiar. Because your mind is so focused on what was and is, the old ways can pull you down into them. But when you continue to use the Eidetic images, your true, freer self emerges naturally.

Carol, a woman in her early 40's when we met, worked as a broker in the highly competitive, male-dominated world of commercial real estate. She was at the height of her business and financial success, yet her body was wracked with pain, and she was

> *"The cost for Carol to excel was a hardening of her spirit, a narrowing of her focus, a pressurized inner landscape that left her tight in body and spirit."*

haunted by thoughts that constantly invaded her mind about how she might be fired by her firm, that she was doing a horrible job, how her male peers were critical of her and perhaps even sabotaged her behind her back. To cope and fit in, she tried to become one of the rough and tumble "good old boys," denying her softer side and playing down her intelligence and insight.

Carol's family suffered a major trauma when she was thirteen. Her parents divorced and father married a neighbor with whom he had been having an affair. His affair shocked everyone in their country club social set and traumatized her younger brother and twin sisters. Carol's mother was unable to support the family financially and their lives were upended after the divorce, creating deep scars for everyone. The children each handled it in their own individual ways. For Carol, it was a *Gone with the Wind* moment: "I'll never go hungry again!" She marshaled all her resources and went from being a mediocre student to later, in college, excelling and focusing on business studies rather than the liberal arts she had enjoyed. Her younger siblings went in the opposite direction—alcohol, drugs, dropping out of school. One brother ended up in jail for theft. The contrast between how Carol coped with trauma and how her siblings coped was extreme.

The cost for Carol to excel was a hardening of her spirit, a narrowing of her focus, a pressurized inner landscape that left her tight in body and spirit. Nothing could ever be enough, because no matter how hard she pushed herself, she couldn't undo the fact that father was gone, mother was miserable, and the whole family was suffering. Internally, Carol felt it was her responsibility for her life never to be upended again. Her answer to achieving that was a tightly wound body, an over-tight focus on climbing the corporate ladder which shut out creativity, accompanied by an underlying sense of desperation driven by fear.

You can well imagine that it was next to impossible for Carol to let go of the stress and pressure she had put on herself to succeed. Just the thought of easing up on herself made her nauseous with a fear that she would lose everything she had gained. She knew the tension was creating disease in her. Her back, shoulders and neck ached and the knots in her muscles never gave way no matter how many chiropractic sessions and massages she had. But she still couldn't let in a moment of internal peace because she was terrified that she'd end up as a broken person like her siblings and her mother.

Like all my clients, Carol began with a Consciousness Mapping which gave me a well-informed idea of which Eidetic images would help her the fastest. The work had to include how to work with her adamant resistance to herself and images that would soften that resistance. Without that work, it would be like putting a bandage on a festering wound, walking away and expecting it to heal.

It was fascinating, and very common that *while she was resisting, she was fully aware of that resistance and could talk about it.* In the moment she was able to access her core, Carol realized that she now had the option of feeling good and basking in the glow of what she was experiencing from inside her. Yet, she rejected it and at that point, she could feel the tug of war between the presence of this oh-so-desired feeling inside of her and her rejection of it.

Eidetic images come from the deeper mind and are not controlled by what we think we *should* see or what we want to see. It's like giving a thoroughbred horse free rein to *move*. When we let our internal thoroughbred that is our natural heritage be free, what we see and feel is surprising. Even shocking. We weren't even aware that we had these parts inside of us.

The Eidetic consciousness, your deeper mind, is highly perceptive and radiates wisdom. Sometimes you feel like laughing at yourself because its messages and gifts are so perfect, and something you never would have come up with from your conscious mind. But that appreciation only comes *after* the resistance has softened.

When I first gave Carol one of her images, designed to bring out hidden and positive parts of her, she *completely rejected her image and the positive feelings about herself that it brought forward.* Her rejection was especially poignant because this image originated *directly from her own mind* during her Consciousness Mapping. Her deeper mind created it. And when she saw it, even knowing that it came from her and was a much needed aspect of herself, she said out loud and insistently, "NO!"

Carol's image was a mythical creature who made her laugh. But she didn't *want* to laugh! She needed to be serious! She needed to be tough! She kept rejecting this creature, and he kept coming back and doing silly things that were fun and playful. Carol did have a very playful side of her, but it had been well hidden. Carol's experience with the image was like when someone makes a joke and you don't want to laugh but it *is* really funny so you laugh despite yourself. It's an odd feeling, somewhere in between pleasure and pain.

Carol was *certain* that this mythical, playful creature was the *last thing* she needed. She watched this image in her mind, operating with a life of its own, as he interacted with her meeting schedule, visually moving meetings with clients around in ways that she had never thought of, but which made her chest relax and gave her an inner lightness. He decorated her dark and somber office with daisies, daffodils and irises, and flung the window wide open to reveal a landscape of spring scents, lush color and delight. He created a thunderstorm that invaded her office building, blowing the roof off and hurling the computers, desks and Carol's smug competitors out of the building into the sunshine. They all walked around dazed but free. He danced around Carol's desk, then sat in her chair with his hooves tapping on her computer screen while smoking a cigar he'd stolen from one of the "old boys."

All of this made Carol chuckle and laugh at herself. Seeing this image was extremely helpful to her. She could actually feel in her body the playful part of her desperate to come out. She could feel how it was helping her feel more ease in herself and at work. And Carol *also* experienced how much she tried to repress and reject this side of herself. This playful image, the repressed part of her, kept coming back no matter how much she tried to squash it or look away. It brought delight and lightness of spirit, slowly uncoiling her body as she watched.

The more Carol watched and allowed this image to have free rein, the looser she became in her body, mind, and soul.

Carol's life was manacled by *no's*. *No's* to more ease at work, to having spaciousness in her life. *No* to being able to perceive herself and others differently. *No* to letting in who she *really* was to replace the soul-sucking self-criticism that haunted her. *No* to connecting with her lover without pushing him aside in impatience because she *had* to work even though she wanted to be with him in her heart. All of these *No's* in her life took her away from herself. Carol couldn't say *yes*, even when she wanted to and even when it served her. She couldn't say *yes* to herself, not even to the parts of her that felt refreshing, real and alive. Well-meaning intelligent suggestions or ideas to improve her work life or schedule would never break through these *nos* in her without dealing with all the ways she resisted herself.

We worked with many different images to ease that *Gone with the Wind* moment of decision which had started her on a path of tension and over-achievement, and which was fed by her feeling that she was never enough. All of her unique core images worked together to reunite Carol with herself, the naturally capable person she was beneath all the layers of crust of her history.

What Carol *naturally* began to express in life was radically different. When she stopped feeling and energetically signaling being tough and unapproachable, other women in her industry felt her openness and spontaneously began to come to her for mentorship. Carol was built for mentoring and enjoyed and excelled in that role. She stopped taking so much work home, and she reorganized and retrained her dysfunctional support staff so they were more capable and empowered which freed up her own time. The freedom she created during her weekends now gave her life instead of draining her. She and her lover made the decision to marry, something which astonished her about herself. Though Carol had stayed away from her mother ever since she left home, Carol now could talk to her mother, be with her and feel close to her. They began to enjoy each other. Chiropractic and massage visits were now more for tuning up her body and pleasure rather than addressing pain.

When a client or patient is seen as particularly "obstinate", a common question from well-meaning therapeutic professionals wanting to break through that barrier is: How are you benefitting from that negative behavior or thinking? What's the benefit to you to keep doing that?

Yes, this question brings you up short. It's jolting! We don't normally perceive negative behaviors as benefitting us. Yet, even though this question is meant to be helpful, it's easy to feel insulted, as if the therapist has misunderstood you. Yes, there is a benefit to many negative behaviors. But really, *if you felt you had a real choice, do you think you would keep doing it even with those benefits?* Most likely not.

Did Carol enjoy operating under mind-bending intensity and self-criticism at work, even though she was successful? Did I really want to follow in my father's footsteps and like him, go bankrupt three times or even once? Absolutely not. To me that well-meaning question is not helpful.

Resistance to change, from my understanding after more than 40 years of working with transformation, must be transmuted. But not by trying to get yourself to be logical. Logic *can* help. But Grand Canyon neural pathways, which are the ones that give us extreme pain, anxiety and suffering, need a different touch.

In DTM, there are several pathways to dissolve your resistance to yourself, and the ones I take with each client are unique to that person. I base each person's pathway on the foundational process of Consciousness Mapping, which is a 1-3 hour experiential tour inside your own mind. It's a bit like living within a riveting and breathtakingly revealing, honest movie of your life.

This movie goes beyond what you've been telling yourself about your life for decades. It goes way beyond what you think about who you are and what is driving you.

It's not magic. It's not metaphor. It's not fantasy.

Once we've discovered, through your personal Consciousness Mapping, where your Grand Canyons of behaviors, feelings and thoughts are, you receive a handful or so of unique core images which address both the way you are repeatedly getting in your own way, and also keys to creating (rediscovering) a more organic way of being. We clear out the debris from your naturally endowed pathways that you may not have used in decades. You begin to naturally operate from your whole self, not the parts of you compressed by your history.

It's *such* a relief.

By connecting to what is *already inside you, even if deeply, seemingly irrevocably buried,* we move the needle from overwhelm to choice, from over-controlled to free, from massive lack of self-confidence, no matter what the evidence says to the contrary, to deep pleasure in simply being you.

Rather than pushing against or trying to logically convince you to change, your inner natural abilities are *able* to come through, because the neural pathways to those choices are now well traveled and become the natural pathways you follow.

The Eidetic images ease your internal resistance by allowing you to repeatedly experience other compelling, real and authentically positive parts of yourself. You soften the aggravating and knee-jerk *no* and instead experience the YES inside you.

Experience for Yourself: Could You Say Yes?

Name three ways or areas in which you frequently say "no." For example, your boss invites you to increase your visibility and credibility by writing a chapter in a book and you refuse. Your partner wants to relocate, and you won't discuss it. You love to travel and your best friend wants you to join her for a European trip but you're always too busy.

Is there *any* way that saying *yes* to those areas would serve you? Have loved ones urged you to try something different? Have you felt an inkling from deep inside you that maybe your relationship or career could be better? Have you noticed how it seems like you say a lot of Nos?

This reflection can help to crack open the door, especially if you are becoming more aggravated by yourself, or afraid of the negative consequences to yourself of what you are doing.

Would you like to go beyond a reflection exercise and get more into the nitty gritty of how you are resisting yourself? Here's a great way to do that—and discover your unique resistances and very possibly some relief you didn't know was possible. www.WendyYellen.com/DTMBook

Stage Seven:
Practice and Reinforcement

"Effort isn't a war with destiny. Destiny itself has imposed on us this effort."

~ Rumi, 13th century Persian poet

Y ou've had a lifetime of "practice" traveling down your old neuropathways. It makes sense that you need practice to reinforce and strengthen your organic but previously hidden pathways. What exactly *do* we practice, and how do we reinforce your gains in the DTM system?

Instead of deciding you must think a different way or just do your best to make yourself not feel bad, in DTM, you get to actually feel better about yourself every time you use the method correctly. Practice and reinforcement re-establish and magnify the organic, authentic you, the you without the crust of your history.

Frequent periods of three to five minutes each, spent in your unique core images, do the work *for* you. You don't need to spend hours at a time, you don't need time to "integrate" or "process" because your images open up the more positive neuropathways without your *conscious* assistance. There is nothing to integrate, nothing outside of you to get used to because you are not bringing a *new* piece of yourself. Instead, you are connecting with the best of you that has been there all along, but has remained unknown to you because it was buried by your history. There is nothing to process because it simply feels like the real you coming out, unexpectedly and delightfully.

It's as natural and stunning as the ability to heal physically. Just as we have the natural capacity for physical healing, we also have that same capacity to heal emotionally. We only feel the need to manipulate ourselves to change because we don't know or believe that our authentic Self is still there. She has all the healing power and answers we need. She just needs an opening, an invitation so she can re-emerge on her own, in her own way, as herself.

After decades of working with deep transformation, and the experience of thousands of my clients, I *know* that we already contain the seeds of our own transformation. It's simply a question of how to find those seeds, how to nourish, water and fertilize them, so they can grow. Despite lip service to the idea, many people no longer believe we have what we need within. Whether you fully believe it from the beginning of your work or not, by using Eidetic images, you *can* get to those parts of your consciousness so they can thrive.

This natural feeling of change is what happens when the authentic you emerges from your history, unfettered. Time spent in and with your Eidetic images and the DTM process creates the change, and you emerge.

Think about this for a moment: It's normal to have some difficulties with our parents at some stage of growing up. Who your mother was with you was determined by her history and the ways her parents were with her, which is determined by their history, and so on. Take for example my mother's need to be perfect, which hurt her badly and which I swallowed whole.

My mother was many things and being hard on herself was just one of them. But it was part of who she was raising me: I felt her harshness towards herself, and unconsciously learned from it how I should also be. That was the mother I had wired into me.

Over time through honestly revisiting my images and grappling with my resistance to feeling different, I felt deeply satisfying, softening, unwinding experiences of me with a softer, less conflicted, kinder and warmer mother. This repeated experience was as visceral as if it were happening now, which, neurologically, it was. My inner tensions unwound. Being with *this mother* gave me *the experience* of being with a mother who was NOT perfectionistic, NOT distant, NOT judgmental. Being with *this mother* allowed me to feel much freer, more loved, more loving. *I* grew softer with *this* mother.

Then a surprising softening happened that was inspired by one of my Mastermind clients. The Mastermind is my program that is by invitation only. It's for clients who have learned through experience that they can *trust* their process and *trust* their images. Most importantly, they continue to work with their core images because they *know* their deeper self will take them where they want to go, even, and especially, when it feels challenging.

In one Mastermind three-day retreat, we worked extensively with the ways that the historical mother, the mother we experience as the mother we actually had, can be softened in real, natural and profound ways.

One woman in particular understood how important this specific work was for her, and how much it would help her. She worked with the tools from the retreat frequently and the results were obvious—and inspiring—to everyone, including me. This is a powerful aspect of co-consciousness and the Eidetic Mastermind: As one person evolves and expands, she brings everyone up with her.

Witnessing her speed of change, I resolved to go even more into my personal core images with the tools from that retreat. And because I did that, I experienced my mother as I *never had before*, even though I have been working with my Eidetic images for almost two decades.

Instead of having a deep experience of her as *not* perfectionistic and *not* tense, I *experienced her, as real as if it were happening in real life*, as open, flowing, magical, mystical, kind, full of deep generosity of spirit and moving through her life, and mine, touching me with all of those qualities and gracing me with them too.

Feeling *this* mother, being with *this* mother, was something I had never felt in my entire life. Being with her eased me, softened me, softened the lines in my face, made me feel loved, whole, and magical and mystical myself.

My mother had those qualities. They had peeked through and I had seen them. I was able to *experience as if it were happening to me* the way she always was with newborn infants and with her stroke patients, so soft and loving and gentle. She was also creative and had the gift of bringing beauty to everything she did. But to *experience her in my bones like that was a gift.*

When you experience your parent with *their* gifts, instead of their history, it loosens something in you. Something you hadn't even known was tight. And with that loosening comes a present *and a future* where *that* version of you is more contactable, more in charge, more present, than you thought possible. Experiencing this you can be felt at the cellular, chemical level as it would have been had you experienced this from birth.[10]

This depth of transformation comes with staying with the process and reinforcing the opening of the neural pathways, even when part of you doesn't think you can. Once, on a particularly difficult day of feeling peevish and grappling with myself, I asked Dr. Ahsen how often and how long I needed to work with my images to have the changes I wanted. He quietly answered, "It's your banquet, you can return and partake as often as you like."

---

10   The depth of the change feels like it is at the developmental level. It is as if you are actually being reparented. It is that powerful.

Stage Eight:
Naturally Experience the Real You

"What makes the desert beautiful," said the little prince, *"is that somewhere it hides a well..."*

~Saint-Exupéry, *The Little Prince*

How can you experience a feeling or opening in an Eidetic image for something that didn't happen "in real life"? How can that be real or true when you know darn well you didn't experience it that way in your life? Isn't that just a fantasy? No. But your historical self wants to fight to keep things the same, no matter how bad it feels.

The final stage in the Deep Transformation Method™ is, like all the stages, woven into a sweetly scented braid where each part weaves under and through all of the others. The entire process feeds your body, mind and soul from the moment you begin the process *in earnest.* How can that be? Because it is so delicious to return to your true self, to feel like you live in your own skin, to make decisions from your elegant mind, rather than from pettiness, envy, exhaustion or carelessness. My psychologist friend Barry Elkin calls it "choosing to live like a mensch[11] rather than through your psychopathologies." Or, as Paul Watzlawick quipped, "Maturity is doing what you think is best, even when your mother thinks it's a good idea."

The difference is that this is not *choosing* to live a certain way. You come from within yourself, gracefully unleashed.

Another aspect of experiencing the real you is that you are experiencing yourself not only without all the layers of your history suffocating you, but also without your *resistance* to yourself. This is one of the oddest concepts and experiences I've had with Eidetics, and one which my clients love because it's so desired, so real, and so unexpected. Stage Eight continues to soften your resistance to yourself, because that part of our nature is so strong and can be

11 Yiddish for a person of noble character and integrity

so destructive to our dreams.

Susan was in her late 40's when we met by video call for an introductory private session. She is a graceful, lithe, kind-eyed woman, but her face and body were tense with strain. At the pinnacle of her law career, she had accolades, financial success, recognition and one of the top positions in her specialty field, a specialty which required an intense amount of analytical ability. Yet, she felt like a complete fraud all of the time. She was absolutely certain that she didn't measure up intellectually. She was sure her colleagues would discover how little she really knew and throw her out. In law firm meetings, she never stopped judging what was coming out of her mouth and was sure it was drivel. Because of this, she worked even longer hours than her peers, edited and re-edited her work, pressuring herself constantly.

She kept her lover at arm's length while also needing and wanting love and closeness. Her body, understandably, began to shut down in strange and mysterious ways. She was exhausted, harried, upset and longed for the time in her past when she had made time for herself, for yoga, her artistic pursuits, and meditation. That time was barely even a distant memory now.

Susan was afraid she would never feel like herself again. Workshops, retreats, and therapy over the years helped. But nothing resolved the way she felt about herself. Nothing stopped her constant comparing herself to others and always coming up short. Nothing lessened the intensity of the stress she felt. As with most things emotional, there were multiple historical beginnings for her stress and her extreme lack of self-confidence.

In this first meeting, after explaining more about what she was facing and what she wanted instead, I took her through three different Eidetic experiences. In the first Eidetic image, her deeper mind showed her an image of her young self alone, vulnerable, scared and forgotten. She felt naked and so alone. The feelings she had from seeing this Eidetic image were deep, troubling and *very* familiar. Because they were familiar to her *now*, and important and troubling to her, I knew we were in the right place.

What she saw was not a memory per se, but something her mind naturally revealed. She didn't try to create something. It arose naturally when I suggested she feel her current stressful feelings and allow an image to arise. This aspect of the work, not having to create something with her conscious mind, was a relief and a release for her. She didn't need to "do" anything and that resonated with her.

Her image came with painful feelings that she often felt as an adult and had also felt when she was younger. It was clear that she needed a way out of those feelings. But this process isn't about changing those painful feelings by understanding them, rationalizing them, processing them, or using the conscious mind to "fix the problem" in any way. What DTM and Eidetics seek to contact is the Self *below* the painful feelings, which is who you are organically, before the constrictions from history, family, society, and religion are imposed on you. We don't want to *bypass* the feelings, but to reach down, grab the Self who has hidden underneath those feelings for all these decades, and bring her back, fully formed and with all her genetic potentials.

This is who you really are beneath the crust of your history.

And the "problem" you keep encountering actually holds the key to more of you, to the solution you keep looking for, while all the time thinking "if only I could get rid of the problem."

The problem IS your solution.

To begin to reach that buried but very much alive self, we went into an Eidetic image called Emanations. This image powerfully brings forward aspects of us that are still there, even though they have been hidden from us by our history. In Susan's image, her younger self who was so alone and sad got up, grew older, and walked into a forest, feeling and looking light, strong and confident. This Eidetic image was not wishful thinking or fantasy. Susan did not decide to rescue herself. Instead, the image came unbidden and unguided from deep within her. I could see the change in her face and body as she did this. Her neck elongated, lines of strain eased in her face, and her eyes looked unveiled.

Susan loved this unusual and much desired experience of herself as healthy and strong. But I could see (and she agitatedly also told me) that she still felt shackled in her image just as she did in her life. She felt partially released. But now that she had some relief, the remaining constraints felt even worse. She had tasted freedom and thus became more aware of the shackles. She strained to get out from under them. Now that she could feel what was *her* and *not* her, she was eager for more. But she also questioned and doubted that she could get there.

When an image has partially released someone, it's always possible to continue and find a way to go even deeper, for fuller release and contact with the self. I suggested yet another Eidetic image, one designed to open Susan up even more. The specifics of what she saw next and the accompanying feelings again came directly from her deeper mind without any controlling or predetermining of what she saw.

In her next image, she was in a roomful of her male colleagues, but this time retaining the experience of natural confidence. "I feel radiant." As she said this, she looked astonished at herself. The experience was taking her places she didn't consciously think were accessible to her. At this point the feelings and sensations of radiance and confidence were visible in her face and body, and palpable for her. She was actually having the sensations of confidence, the chemicals of the feeling of confidence, coursing through her body in the moment. This chemical shift is why the experience felt so visceral and compelling to her. It also supports the ability of neuroplasticity in your brain to change because you are experiencing aspects of yourself that are real, and you are feeling them pop up and stream through your body and mind.

This chemical shift happens when you use DTM and the tool of Eidetics in part because you are not simply thinking or trying to rearrange your feelings. You are accessing that deeper part of you. Once you contact this part, it feels real because it *is* real.

Since she was eager, willing and also surprised and engaged in what was coursing through her, I then helped her deepen her image even further. You can return to an image, hours later, days later, even years later and wring even more goodness for yourself simply by immersing yourself in the image and letting it take you by the hand to where it naturally wants to go. Images change, subtly and not so subtly, over minutes, and over years.

When a Certified Eidetic Practitioner with the skills, experience and training to stay with the image and not impose herself onto the client's experience works on an image with you, you can usually go much further and deeper as you dive into your psyche. It's always helpful not to go it alone. Because even though you are working to feel better, it does take courage. You are going beyond what is familiar and what *feels* true. And easing past the barrier of what you've always assumed to be you, to feeling your authentic self, feels odd *and* rather strange—and at the same time, totally known.

Deepening the image increases your contact with your Self and allows the power of your experience to shift the neural pathways so that you organically begin to *live* even more of the changes in the image. This is essential for real change and transformation to occur.

As we spent more time seeing the image of Susan with the roomful of her male colleagues, she went from a radiant feeling of matter of factly presenting information to them to a feeling of *compassionately and creatively* teaching. She was presenting not only from her newly accepted formidable intellect but also from her newly unleashed *heart and creative side*. The presence and power of these combined with her intellect stunned, amazed and delighted her. It also *clearly* delighted and entranced the men in the image. Rather than being brow-beaten through the force of logic and academic arguments, they were swayed by her softer, more open approach.

What man, what person, wouldn't prefer to be creatively, compassionately taught in a way that opens them to their own heart, creativity and abilities, over being lectured by intellect alone? Susan was sharing from her deeper self. It was not just her information but also her way of being that gave the men room and space to move, to grow, to connect with something beyond their analytical minds. This created a workplace that allowed for and complimented growth and pleasure, not just success. Taking her skills and her colleagues in this direction had never been in her mind, but she was delighted with it, and with herself, and the results at work proved the wisdom of her deeper mind.

This open, expansive, connected part of Susan was the place in her that was available to her at all times. This deeper part expressed the qualities she had resisted for decades because they felt dangerous due to her family history and also dangerous in an intensely competitive, male-dominated workplace that worshipped analysis and intellect alone. She thought allowing her heart and creative side to show would be a recipe for disaster.

Conventional wisdom tells women like Susan that the masculine, super-analytical world will run over you if you are too vulnerable, if you dare to come from your heart as well as your intellect. Lawyers are trained to be tough, competitive, sharp, analytical and to portray invulnerability at all times. You can well imagine that being a vulnerable lawyer with a softer, creative approach may not look like the fastest route to success. Still, by complying with that conventional wisdom, Susan had rejected an important, more creative, softer side of herself which she desperately needed—not just for success, but also for her love relationship, her body's health and for regaining any sense of wholeness.

As she regained contact with this vulnerable, heart-felt, creative side without losing any of her confidence, intelligence or strengths, Susan knew to the core of her being that she no longer needed to bury parts of herself in order to be more successful. That feeling of being gracefully unleashed walks right into your life, sits down, smiles graciously, and offers you a cup of tea.

Be clear that I was not trying to get Susan to relax or open her heart or express her creativity. I was simply guiding her through *her* deeper mind to get to what was buried inside her and struggling to come out. I had no preconceptions or idea of what would or should happen. I did know, and trust, that whatever came out would be more of *her*. And that is what she was looking for. For other clients, it would have been *other* aspects of the self. The beauty of this work is that it's not cookie cutter. Every person's work is unique to them.

In our time together, Susan went on to repair her tattered relationship with her father and brother, successfully tackle a variety of complicated health issues, and feel love and tenderness towards her lover.

Even years later, Susan still embraces these parts of herself that had come out in our very first work together. In fact, she used this image of herself over and over for years to strengthen access to this heart-centered, creative and refreshingly curious part of herself. Using this image to access those parts of herself, she also won a multi-million-dollar law client, one which her analytically-focused colleagues had failed to procure. The part of her she had resisted was exactly what she needed more of.

We *think* we need to act a certain way—in love, in relationships, at work, in business. But the ways we *think* we need to act are also controlled by our history. We acted this way often in history, so it feels familiar and seems right. Or our parents acted a certain way, and though it was disastrous for them, it again feels at least *somewhat* right because we know these patterns and they feel like a comfortable well-worn shoe. However, when our history is no longer controlling us, when the ways we think and feel and behave are no longer coming from our history and constricted ways of being, the organic self naturally emerges.

For your own unique Eidetic experience, including Emanations, which Susan loved and so brilliantly moved her forward, go here: www.WendyYellen.com/DTMBook.

Unexpected Gifts:
Love, Empathy, Intuition and Spiritual Connection

In working with the DTM process as they delve into the deeper part of the mind that is not controlled by expectations and over-analysis, most of my clients discover four surprise gifts that come packaged together. You may not have these gifts at the top of your list of what you hoped to accomplish by this work. You are no doubt more concerned in resolving what is so painful right now. But once clients have received these gifts, they are often amongst the most cherished. These gifts appear on their own, simply from the process of accessing this deeper part of your mind where the Eidetic consciousness dwells.

These gifts are: a heart open to love, natural access to empathy, increased intuition, and a deeper, more accessible spiritual connection.

You may not be interested in this aspect of what can happen in you and for you, and then again, you may be. I mention them because these gifts come unbidden, naturally, when you have quieted down the conscious part of the mind and are able to take a chair, sit by the river of your mind, and feel some peace.

Perhaps even the mention of contact with something greater touches sore points in you, or doesn't match with your beliefs, or even turns you off. If so, I understand that this section is absolutely not for everyone. If you feel that way, please skip over what doesn't connect with you. I believe that there is *something* in this chapter for everyone. But not *everything* in it is for everyone. It's yours to pick and choose what is right for you.

Love

"Love and compassion are like the weak spots in the walls of ego. They are like a naturally occurring opening. And they are the opening we take. If we connect with even one moment of good heart or compassion and cherish it, our ability to open will gradually expand."

~ Pema Chödrön, Buddhist nun

Janet had given up on her marriage in all but name. There was so little contact between her part of the house and her husband's that her home felt like two castles separated by a moat. Their lives sailed past each other, ships in the foggy night, without even fog horns to announce the other's presence. Her life was full. Their children had launched into careers and relationships which meant she and Robert felt little pull to arrange the warming blanket of life over both of their laps.

Janet was so far beyond caring that she was way beyond even feeling resigned. Other parts of her life kept her alive and engaged. Her flute and the community chamber orchestra she played in created a rich, satisfying life. Janet's list of what she wanted from our DTM work together didn't even include Robert.

Janet wasn't taking good care of her health, despite several close calls with cancer. She felt angry and distant from her 92-year-old mother, which was uncomfortable and complicated because she was the only sibling living near her mother's assisted living center. To bring Janet more into contact with herself, we worked on early childhood traumas from her father's depression and drinking, and her mother's not-quite-hidden affairs. Janet felt angry and unseen as a child growing up. Her parents' difficulties left them with little energy to spare for Janet, who they thought was a good kid and seemed to take care of herself.

In the early childhood trauma work, we went back to unearth

and bring forward the child who strived to look okay when she wasn't. It wasn't simply the anger and being ignored that haunted her. What was missing inside was even more important and powerful: Janet's ability to play the leading role in her own life. Janet wanted, and needed, to have an impact, to matter, to show up, to be comfortable in the limelight with all her talents on display. Instead, she tried to seem okay when she wasn't. She tried to make herself small when she was in fact a guiding force that the world, and especially her world, needed.

For years Janet had wanted to join the more prestigious orchestra in her large city but hadn't felt good enough to even audition. This despite the accolades and high praise she received whenever her community orchestra performed. After working with the Eidetic images, Janet felt empowered to reach out. She auditioned and began to play in the orchestra as a substitute and later became their principal flutist. Coming out with her talents this way, and feeling recognized and seen, was something Janet celebrated in herself. She also felt proud to model that empowerment for her own children.

Two things then happened unexpectedly. Janet's husband Robert began attending her concerts and spontaneously initiated a weekly date night, something he had never even broached before. To say Janet was stunned would be the understatement of the millennium! She hadn't opened her heart to him, or her body, for many decades, and hadn't thought of him as a partner. He gently but persistently moved towards her. It was as if his heart had bloomed open and repeatedly presented scented, lush bouquets to her timidly receptive but still partially closed heart.

Janet also began to receive him in the spirit with which he was opening to her. They changed the functions of certain his-her rooms of their sprawling home to rooms they could share. He could read and watch his favorite shows while she raised her violets and sketched portraits. They were no longer ships passing in the night. Both of them were astonished because they were already in their 60s and reconnecting had been a hope that had died long ago. Did this take some effort for Janet? Did she have to become aware of the ways that habit had kept her locked down and kept her away from Robert in body, mind and spirit? Yes. But now she was more than willing. She was eager for more of him. Her desire to renew that part of herself guided her through the uncomfortable, challenging parts of his newfound openness.

Janet and I never focused on her marriage because it wasn't even on her list. But when the overly critical, locked-into-history part of the self is calmed down, and when the repressed inner Self begins to breathe, the heart opens automatically and love comes gently in. Robert had felt Janet's softening and was responding to that unspoken but clear invitation.

Love. Once you step out of the control of the conscious, rational mind and allow yourself to receive what comes from the Eidetic consciousness, this is one of the gifts that pour in. The gifts come in large part because you are accessing something deeper in yourself, a part of you that is naturally more open and more alive. It's you without the constraints of your history. Think of an infant in your arms. That face, that smile, those open, unshielded eyes. That is who we are before history shapes us. Love comes pouring into those eyes. Love and delight come pouring out.

Then the destructive machinery of history comes rumbling in, with its constraints, threats, expectations, and traumas which start to create us in their image. We lose some of our fun and our sassy square edges in order to fit into the round holes of plodding expectations created by family, society, school, religion.

But as the crust of history starts to crumble away it reveals the heart. Instead of what we think we must say and do and feel, instead of what we were trained to do, instead of being one step removed from life, we now access the moment itself. Not every moment, of course not. But more and more and more.

This change in a marriage is very common in my work even

with women who have been disconnected from their partner for decades, and who have resigned to orbiting in different universes. Perhaps because the distance has gone on for so long, they have an unspoken, unexamined acceptance of the status quo and they feel nothing can be done. They choose to direct their energy to other, seemingly more promising situations. They have no belief, and in some ways, no desire, to have their marriage be any different. And yet, it's a deadening life for both partners. It also can be deadening, alarming, and future-predictive for the children.

"But if words do not reach the ear in the chest, nothing happens."

~ Rumi, 13th century Persian poet

After years of working with Eidetics, I made a conscious decision that I wanted to live in a *house of love* with my husband Michael. We had been with each other for decades, but my mind had a permanent seat on the hamster wheel of criticism and judgment. Being naturally hard on myself, I unwittingly also made him a target for my perfectionism. This roiling stream of negativity set up roadblocks against giving and receiving love. What we had then was not a house of love, though there was still much love in it. I wanted to create this house and was not asking him to do it with me. I did it as a practice for me, because that is who I wanted to be. It was my lesson to unravel, and I also knew it would change us both.[12] Opening to love and opening to Spirit, for me, are the same. When you become less controlled by your automatic reactions to life, to your loved ones, to yourself, love rushes in.

It's natural because you repeatedly connect with and embrace your deeper Self, and that deeper Self knows more than you

12 There are theories of change and relationship that would disagree and instead would expect both people to actively participate in creating a shift. But for me it was the spiritual practice of love that I wanted and needed for myself, with the knowing that both he and the marriage would also change if I could operate less from history, loosen my negative identification with my mother's perfectionism, and open myself to love.

consciously know. You stop erecting barriers of expectations, insistent blindness and need for control over the uncontrollable between you and yourself, between you and the feelings in your heart.

Empathy

"Everybody you know, you see, you remember, you will meet, is another face of God, is another doorway through."

~ Ram Dass

In writing about love and the heart, empathy (love's sister), always comes along for the ride. When we feel a real empathic understanding or knowing of another person, we are automatically standing in their shoes, looking through *their* eyes, and experiencing what they think and feel. We are no longer restricted to our own narrow vision of what we think is real and who we believe they are. Eidetics deepens our ability to experience this empathic connection to someone else.

One client in her late 40s comes strongly to mind because this moment shocked me. She was talking about her recent vacation and a museum exhibit, and as she described a woman near her, my client used one of the most vicious racist comments I had ever heard anyone speak out loud. I grew up in a home where I never heard my parents say anything racist or derogatory about any group of people. In fact, they both went out of their way to be kind and that's what they taught us to do. I was also raised Jewish, so I have a special antenna for prejudice and slurs.

Her words shocked me but especially because these words came from *her*, and I knew her to be an outspoken but also generous-minded woman. The way she matter-of-factly said the slur made me wonder if perhaps she didn't realize how extremely belittling and unkind it was.

It seemed impossible that she *wouldn't* know. Still, it was an ugly insult and nothing she had ever said or done had shown her to be that kind of person.

She certainly hadn't come to me to deal with her prejudices. But I knew her well enough to know she would be grateful to me for not assuming she meant to be unkind. After I gently broached the subject, she confirmed that she hadn't thought at all about what she said or how she perceived this group of people. With her surprised but eager permission and trust, we worked with an Eidetic image exercise that automatically allows one person to understand and/or *take in* the point of view of another person.

Once she truly understood what she had said, she burst into tears, shocked at her own cruelty. Years later she told me a story of casually meeting a woman from the same ethnic group as the woman at the museum. She remembered our work together, and she had an especially meaningful conversation with this woman. She said she hoped in some way she was healing the scar that her thoughtlessness had created in the world. She had understood *empathically* how a stranger might feel.

As we know *ourselves* more deeply we automatically see and feel others as who *they* really are. This openness to Self lets others in and is deeply satisfying and richly connecting. You cannot know another person well when your history is blocking what you experience and controlling your expectations and responses. Knowing ourselves well, without blinders, allows us to be with others in a way that wasn't even hinted at before.[13]

Often in the Mastermind, a client shares an image and several other members see specifics in the image that the client saw but hadn't specifically shared. The images have an integrity of their own and can be seen and felt by others who are looking (and not

13 Thank you to Dr. Barbara Goldman and Dr. Mark Glat for highlighting this for me—synchronistically just two days apart.

just thinking about what they are seeing). This kind of contact with someone else is a rare gem. The person sharing their image feels seen and heard on an almost unknown level. The person watching another's image is giving the precious gift of themselves and their empathy.

As you dwell more in this Eidetic level of consciousness, the mind is automatically quieted, and you receive a new kind of information about yourself, others, and about life.

Go here for your own experience of this level of empathic connection: www.WendyYellen.com/DTMBook.

"So come, my friends, be not afraid! We are so lightly here! It is in love that we are made. In love we disappear."

~Leonard Cohen

Spiritual Connection and Intuition

"Leaning into that rawness is not my first inclination, but when I stay with my direct experience, I begin to feel fluid and non-bounded, as if my molecules are mixing with clear space, as if there is no distinction between me and not me. An openness arises, a calmness."

~ Geneen Roth

This section is not about religion. It's about your relationship and connection with something larger, which goes by many names—God, Spirit, Source, the Universe, the Divine, Universal energy, Jesus, Allah, Yahweh. If deepening your contact with Spirit interests you, this section is for you. If not, simply skip over it.

Every text about spirituality speaks to the human desire for contact with Spirit and the importance of love and offers ideas for how to open up to experience something greater than ourselves.

How can we soften the ways we interfere with that ever-present possibility of contact with Source and with love?

One way we interfere is through our overly analytical, overly judgmental mind. When the mind is overactive, it shuts out the whispers of Source. The mind is too loud, too closed.

My experience is that intuition and spirituality are both automatically enhanced through the simple process of accessing this deeper level of ourselves. For example, one of several Eidetic images I use helps to soften the distance certain clients feel that they *have* to create between themselves and nurturing of any kind, even as an adult. It allows them to create a deeper and undisturbed, nurturing connection to the maternal.

Many people think they need to fight against connecting with the maternal, because it was dangerous when they were young— emotionally, physically, psychically. But in this specific image, you dwell in and richly savor the oceanic feeling of early contact with the maternal (your mother without *her* history), without the disturbance from your history. Your body then receives the chemicals of early nurturing, and they course through you.[14] This experience of contact and love softens body tensions and tightly coiled defenses. That softening opens you in many ways, to people and to contact with something Greater.

My client Cheryl was in her early 50s. She had experienced massive early trauma, including a series of hospitalizations before she was five years old.

Her mother's severe depression led to at least one suicide attempt. The stillbirth of what would have been a younger sibling left young Cheryl feeling alone and drifting. The religion of her

14   https://www.aspeninstitute.org/publications/the-brain-basis-for-integrated-social-emotional-and-aca-demic-development/ For a fascinating well-sourced review of the science of early learning and how it relates to neuroplasticity.

youth felt harsh to her and brought her no comfort. She perceived that the world was a dangerous place and used the protection of brittle emotional armor to navigate the world.

She only felt totally safe when she was alone. Books and art became her refuge. She threw herself into both, creating a world of beauty and richness, then locking herself inside of it. The only way she knew to self-soothe was being alone in her room, sitting on her bed encircled by her treasured books, frayed-with-love stuffed animals and paints. The walls of her tiny bedroom were layered with pentimento sketches, penciled outlines of shadows of plants, painted windows into other worlds, layers of her life one atop the other, a magic room of safe aloneness. Outside of her room she had no idea how to feel safe with others.

Feeling betrayed and disappointed by the religion she was raised in, Cheryl often said, "God and I are no longer on speaking terms." Yet her art, animals and her books took her deep into herself, and into contact with something larger than herself that she could not name. That's where she felt safe. *But this safety also* took her *away* from herself, because in isolation she couldn't offer her gifts to the world. She couldn't find her way to be herself while also being in the world. The external world did not feel safe and she closed her true self down in order to function there.

Cheryl dug deep into our work together. She hadn't noticed before that the way she made herself feel safe was also punishing to her body and distancing people from her. This awareness came with pain as she took in the difference between who she thought she was being and how she actually came across. But she didn't close her eyes, she didn't reject what she was noticing about herself.

This willingness became an opening to much more of her and, to her surprise, to more connection with a new sense of Spirit, different from the God she had long ago abandoned. She began to feel safe in her own skin. She no longer had to close down and hide herself away to feel okay. As she came out into the world *with* her spiritual connection, her young adult daughters opened more to her, sharing their own journeys. As her daughters created families and birthed babies of their own, this sharing took on an even deeper pleasure and meaning for Cheryl.

"Before I experienced myself as a pylon driver. I felt rigid and claustrophobic. Then when we opened me up to my deeper self, a sweeter, softer Presence was beside me. It felt like the Gardens of Babylon, filled with the scent of fresh pine, dates and pears."

My spiritual opening has been similar. I had practical worries that I wanted to address with the Eidetic images. What fascinated me was that as I worked through more of my resistance against myself, as I stopped relying only on my overly analytical mind, my connection to Source and trust of that connection automatically grew.

When I met Dr. Ahsen the very first time, none of his work, Eidetics, made even a drop of sense to me. I fought against it so hard I could barely even hear a word he said, my mind was screaming so loud, and I went away from that first workshop shaking my head. What was everyone so excited about? Later, desperate for some relief, I worked with Eidetics during a crisis in my life. It helped me but it still didn't make any sense. I certainly couldn't have described to you what I was doing or why. But it gave me exactly what I needed, and I felt better, even if I didn't understand it.

Years later, I attended an Introduction to Eidetics workshop that Dr. Ahsen led but this time I felt like I had found the Holy Grail. I was hooked. Despite decades of working on myself with all kinds of traditional and non-traditional therapies and therapists, when I worked with him, I immediately experienced my resistance to a more satisfying life *right there*, sitting on a couch in a roomful of strangers. And I could feel the opening in me too, even though I fought against it. This work, Eidetics, seemed to be what I had been hoping was possible, and why I had kept my hope alive. Finally!

Contact with something Greater, a spiritual connection, was absolutely not in my mind or priorities *at all*. I had very pressing concerns which I wanted to ease and that's all that I thought about.

But over the years, as my mind quieted and my resistance softened, I connected more easily to what had become important to me—a deeper knowing and deeper spiritual connection. I began to more easily hear and feel beyond the immediately obvious. I'd always valued my intuition, and I *loved* synchronicities, but now I had developed a level of trust in myself and in what was coming to me. Small pieces of contact, in different ways, arose often, not rarely as they had before.

At first, I didn't trust it. I know that sometimes fear can warp intuition. We mistake our fears, which are shaped by our past, for intuitive knowing. When we mistake fear for intuitive knowing while we're making decisions, it often brings us to a *no* rather than a *yes*. Your intuitive self, when you are clear of historical repetition, is a different guidance system from your feelings. It's very helpful to be able to distinguish intuition from old feelings that *feel like* intuition but aren't.

My mind had always worked hard to be in control, and I didn't feel I could trust this knowledge that was coming to me in large part because it came with no prior evidence or careful analysis. Yet when I gave myself permission to follow an intuitive hit with a client or myself, time after time it was wise beyond anything I had "thought." Often the results of following those intuitive hits took my client, and me, to unexpected but deeply immersive states of awe. And so, my trust grew. As my trust grew, guidance came in more often, I listened faster, and the trickle became a spring.

My intuitive knowing, my trust of the information coming to me, delightful synchronicities—all of these came braided together as a whole. I was letting more love in with my husband, but that also came with a bigger heart all around, including in my relationship with Spirit. Before I did this work, I didn't really *have* a relationship with Spirit, at least not one that I was aware of. Now it feeds me, and opens me more, especially in my heart. It's a path I choose to continue travelling on.

Part of this knowing comes from contact with the Eidetic mind. When "listening eidetically" to a client, or watching their image, information becomes available that is in their images, even if I'm not aware of it consciously. Sitting with a question and opening to guidance, listening to it and being willing to follow it while respecting it as a gift was a massive challenge initially. I realize that not everyone would agree with me that this level of contact is more than just my many years of experience that brings a kind of knowing. For me, I experience it as contact with something larger than me, a wisdom and perception that I didn't know I had, awe, and appreciation. You may not call it spiritual, but I hope you recognize the special feeling in what I am describing which, when it happens, brings a feeling of tender heartedness, arising unbidden, and which takes the breath away.

A beautiful example of spiritual connection and opening happened for a client *during* the writing of this chapter. Now *that* is synchronicity! Laurie came to me wanting to enhance her spiritual connection and she sees the world as offering her opportunities to do that. But as with all of us, it's an opportunity that sometimes feels like climbing Mt Everest during an ice storm. In Eidetics, for those who want it, we have images specifically designed to open you to contact with something greater. During the session, she opened more to her natural state of trust, which lies beneath her history but sometimes gets obscured. As we ended, she said with quiet conviction: "I love this. I feel good, ready for whatever comes, very receptive, I'll be guided, supported. I feel transcendent love."

Eidetics and DTM have real value for meditators and others interested in deepening their spiritual life. Amongst the thousands of Eidetic images that release developmental obstacles and resolve trauma, there are also specific Eidetic images which open you even more to your spiritual life, however *you* define that. In my experience, though, *every* Eidetic and DTM experience opens you more on that level. It's simply that some specific images create that opening purposely.

"That which flares up inside you is not madness but the flame of life itself. You must fulfill it and live for it 'til you are free."

-Akhter Ahsen

A Final Word

I have only given you a taste of the DTM process and Eidetics and the gifts experienced by some of my clients. Unexpected energy, a return of curiosity not felt for decades, trust in the self and in the world, sensuality and playfulness—these qualities arise because they are part of our true, organic nature.

I want you to know what is available, truly available, to everyone who has the desire and the willingness to go there:

Parents often don't recognize that the way they were trying to help their young adult children creates distance and pain. Instead of approaching these young people with faces drawn in gut wrenching worry, my clients were able to take in their child as a person and love and appreciate who they actually are. Hearts opening in both directions.

Many adults have forgotten what energy and curiosity feel like. So when my clients allow themselves to know, feel and finally follow their life-long but buried dreams, what do they experience? Bursting with energy and curiosity as those dreams are unleashed.

I've seen hard-nosed professionals learn to lead their work teams through shark-infested waters with kindness and love—not through effort but with those qualities arising unbidden.

Clients have experienced those few extra seconds of patience and restraint that make all the difference between blasting their aggravation onto the object of their frustration or remembering who this is they are talking to.

Rather than suspicion or blind trust, they find a naturally wise trusting and opening.

I wish these things for you as well.

Warmly,

Wendy Yellen

There are several directions you can take from here:

If you've read this book to understand yourself better, then I encourage you to pick up all the threads and invite them into your everyday life. While awareness alone is not enough for deep transformation, it is a great start.

If you want to experience Eidetics and DTM for yourself, virtually, there are many resources here: www.WendyYellen.com/DTMBook. Instagram: wendy.yellen

Or, if you are someone like me, and you feel a compelling, unquenchable thirst to move forward *now,* you can easily schedule a meeting with me here, my gift to you. www.WendyYellen.com/DTMBook.

When we meet virtually, I'll walk you through an experience of yourself that is different from any other type of transformational work I know of. If this work is for you, and if I am the person you resonate with, then I'll show you how to take the next step. You can start that process here: www.WendyYellen.com/DTMBook.

A Letter To Dr. Ahsen

Dear Dr. Ahsen,

You gave me a beautiful, wise process that I love and that loves me. You gave me the gift of your caring, presence and wisdom.

One Sunday when I was in excruciating pain and bleeding without knowing why, you stayed on the phone throughout the day with me, seeking images that would help me even while I wanted to scream in pain, until finally the pain and the bleeding stopped. And never returned.

When I couldn't get out of my own head, when I was so busy questioning you that I wouldn't let the process in, when my judgmental side was so strong it took over everything, you never gave up on me.

When you were at your wits end after years of me refusing to allow my deeper self to have a chance, and questioning everything without letting it in, you almost fired me as a client. That shocked me, and I recognized then how much I risked losing. Thank you.

When I came to you filled to the brim with intelligence and learning but with no space to open more, and I asked you what to do with a client who perplexed me, you thought awhile and said, "Look at their image." I had been so immersed in my own thinking and trying to solve things in my head that I had forgotten to look at the image.

Thank you for your stories of your Sufi grandfather in the wild forests when you were a boy. Thank you for swimming in the ocean off the coast of Morocco with me. Thank you for showing me a world beyond prejudice, a world of beauty and real possibilities. And especially thank you for giving me the gift of Eidetics which has moved me and my clients beyond what I had ever thought possible.

Acknowledgements

I've been a lover of acknowledgement pages in books for decades. I wonder who the people are in the writer's life and create stories in my mind about them. Now I get to write my own. I saved this page for last - it's daunting and challenging. There are so many people to thank because I've been supported by friends, family, colleagues, teachers, mentors and more… for a lifetime.

For this book, my first, I'm singling out just a few. With a thank you and apology for all of those whose name I did not include but who live with thanks in my heart:

My clients—every single one of you around the world - since 1979. Your trust, your willingness, your honesty with yourself and with me, your courage. And for those of you in my Eidetic Co-Consciousness Groups and Mastermind - your breath-taking generosity with each other. In this book, I so hope you will feel that I told your story (generously mixed with other people's stories to preserve your privacy) in a real and connected and kind way, and that you feel seen, heard, even loved. You are heroes to me. The world is a much better place because you are here.

Mom, Dad, Max, Bungar, Gram and Nella Marion—for shepherding me with so much love, in all your humanity. Visits to the Farm which are some of my best lifetime Eidetic images, with Bowser stories, boys that ride on whale backs in the sea, and books read cover to cover with 3 of us sitting on your lap all sucking our thumbs. And the many years of fresh baked strudel, apple pie with crumb topping, homemade strawberry jam and butternut squash casseroles.

My sister Pamela and my brother Ken—for the past and for the present. I am proud to be your sister and to get to be with who you have each grown up to become.

The Boys—Mark Glat, David Sheslow, Howard Berkman and Bruce Shmilowitz—for serenading me every Thursday afternoon for years and making me laugh and feel seen and appreciated.

Barbara Goldman and Barry Elkin for a lifetime of love.

Rebecca Morasutti for your super powers and your ever-ready magic wand. Having you by my side on this journey has changed everything.

Heather Estay, my first editor ever—what a gift you have of making my writing better, while still standing up for it to be mine. I never knew how good it could feel for someone to have my back. Thank you so much for making this a MUCH better book.

For the women who generously gave their time and energy to give me honest feedback and read this book cover to cover: Liza Fiorentinos, Kelly Hayes and Barbara Goldman, PhD—thank you for that gift!

LJDagnall for shepherding me through my Eidetic images, my obstacles and my insistently blind places with wisdom, kindness, compassion, courage and empathy. And for your generous laugh!

Michael Rogers - the love of my life. You make me laugh, feel seen and loved and though you feel shy about it, I love to hear you sing.